NEW GIRL *on the* JOB

NEW GIRL *on the* JOB

ADVICE FROM THE TRENCHES

HANNAH SELIGSON

FOREWORD BY GAIL EVANS

New York Times best-selling author of
Play Like a Man, Win Like a Woman

CITADEL PRESS
Kensington Publishing Corp.
www.kensingtonbooks.com

CITADEL PRESS BOOKS are published by

Kensington Publishing Corp.
850 Third Avenue
New York, NY 10022

All Kensington titles, imprints, and distributed lines are available at special quantity
discounts for bulk purchases for sales promotions, premiums,
fund-raising, educational, or institutional use. Special book excerpts or
customized printings can also be created to fit specific needs. For details, write or
phone the office of the Kensington special sales manager: Kensington Publishing
Corp., 850 Third Avenue, New York, NY 10022, attn: Special Sales Department;
phone 1-800-221-2647.

CITADEL PRESS and the Citadel logo are Reg. U.S. Pat. & TM Off.

First trade paperback printing: May 2008

10   9   8   7   6   5   4   3   2   1

Printed in the United States of America
Library of Congress Control Number: 2007922594

ISBN-13: 978-0-8065-2943-1
ISBN-10: 0-8065-2943-1

To my Mom, Judy Seligson, a Woman of Valor,
whose love and encouragement made this book happen.

And to my grandmother, Gloria Schaffer,
my role model and heroine,
whose legacy of breaking boundaries inspires me every day.

CONTENTS

FOREWORD

When Hannah Seligson approached me about her idea to write a career guide for young women, called *New Girl on the Job*, I was heartened to see a new generation taking on the issue of how to help women succeed.

When I was a guest on *Larry King Live* in 2003 to talk about my first book, *Play Like a Man, Win Like a Woman*, Larry asked me, "Do women really still need empowering [in the workplace]?" My answer was: "Yes, women absolutely still need empowering when it comes to their careers." We've come a long way, but we still have a very long way to go.

Having to push women to "go for it" in the workplace seems to be a never-ending issue. No longer is the goal securing a "good job." Today, it's equally about how women feel about work and the companies they work for. Statistics show that more and more women are leaving the traditional workplace behind in favor of starting their own business. Why? Because, despite the advances that have been made, the workplace has been slow to change to accommodate their needs. Today's working women are looking at the big picture. They're looking for ways to move beyond a "job" and into a "career." They're looking for a high quality of life—both in and out of the office.

Hannah Seligson has her finger on the pulse of these issues because she is one of these young women. In this book, she offers working women tangible advice about how to make the workplace work for them. In addition, *New Girl on the Job* touches on subjects that every young woman wants and needs to understand: the mechanics of finding a mentor, figuring out how to ally yourself with your female co-workers, and learning the art of self-promotion. And perhaps most important, this book speaks the language of your generation, in a voice you can trust.

New Girl on the Job is the beginning of your generation's movement toward making the role of women in the workplace even more important. Now is the time to take the next step—to seek out satisfying, fulfilling *careers* rather than existing in humdrum jobs, to start getting paid what you are worth, and to use our strength in numbers not only to propel yourself into a top-level job, but also to continue advocating for equality and change for all women. The groundwork has already been laid by the women who have come before you. Now it's your turn to build upon that foundation, for yourselves, for your co-workers, and for the future. Here's your blueprint for how to do it.

> —Gail Evans
> December 2006
> Retired Executive Vice President, CNN
> Author of *Play Like a Man, Win Like a Woman*
> and *She Wins, You Win*

INTRODUCTION

I don't want to tell you this, but I have to. I got fired from my first job.

Even though it was more than a year ago, I still remember the postfiring twinges of shame, feelings of inadequacy, and certainty that my life had ended before it had begun. The disappointment and despair I felt during my nine months of employment is what ultimately inspired me to write. Now you know how painful it was. It was in this undertaking—in the monumental effort to hone my craft, interview over a hundred amazing women about their experiences in the workplace and cull their wisdom in order to share it with others—that I discovered there are even more valuable lessons about what it means to be the New Girl on the Job than I had originally suspected.

Writing this book helped me put my first job experience in perspective. I see now that I was mismatched for my job, and bullied by my boss. I didn't want to spend the whole day making PowerPoint presentations and doing busywork, yet I had never bothered to ask what my job description was! I was so inexperienced: I wondered, like so many other young people starting out, was my office the way all offices were? Was my supervisor's constant nitpicking the only humanity I could expect from my boss? No one had told me what to expect or how to handle the range of situations I was about to encounter, many of which are common to young people of either sex when they are starting out. But equally as many are specific to young women.

Over the past year, I have had the enormous privilege of interviewing women from a wide range of industries, professions, and backgrounds. My sample consisted of one hundred women aged twenty-two to about thirty, from four major cities—New York, Los Angeles, Washington, D.C., and Chicago. While women from these four cities were the bulk of my sample, I also spoke to a smattering of women from a variety of other locations. Twenty percent of my sample were women of color. Location, race, or job title, however, was not the defining factor in what young women were experiencing at work. Whether I was interviewing financial analysts in New York, assistants at talent agencies in Los Angeles, junior aides to politicians in Washington, D.C., or employees at nonprofits in Chicago, young women were all encountering the same types of workplace issues. Everyone was struggling with the basics (Is it okay to be friends with my boss?) to the more complicated (How do I avoid becoming a doormat?). The women at the lower rungs of the ladder were instrumental in shaping the topics addressed in this book. The voices of Gen X and Y are the fabric of *New Girl on the Job*, as they provide the real-life examples and provide the palpable context to discuss what would have otherwise been theoretical Jane Doe prototypes.

I also interviewed seasoned professionals. They are my "panel of experts," a group of women who have made an enormous impact in their respective field, some of whom have very recognizable names, such as Bobbi Brown, founder and CEO of Bobbi Brown Cosmetics; Soledad O'Brien, CNN correspondent; Fern Mallis, the vice president of IMG Fashion; Gail Evans, best-selling author of *Play Like a Man, Win Like a Woman*; and Tory Johnson, the CEO of Women for Hire and career expert for ABC's *Good Morning America*. In addition, I interviewed other high-level women in every field, ranging from finance to television to the nonprofit sector. I asked these women such questions as, "What did you do at the beginning stages of your career to get you where you are today?" "What are the three pieces of advice you have for young women starting out in the twenty-first-century workplace?" "What are some the pitfalls you see young women fall into at the office?" "How do you think this generation of women can break the glass ceiling?" Fashion designer Diane von Furstenberg boils her "New Girl on the Job" advice down to, "I think it is most important for a girl to work. Even when you have a family, it is recommended to have an identity outside of your family. My advice to women is to pay attention to details, put your heart and enthusiasm into work, and just go for it! Enjoy the ride!"

Interviewing such a wide range of women—from those who have "been there"—to those who are "there" in the trenches right now, figuring it out as they go along—gave me the perspective I wish I had had during my short tenure at my first job and perspective that has helped me get where I am today. Perspective I want to pass on to you.

Based on my research, I've also identified lists of takeaways, do's and don'ts, and other helpful guideposts to give you the information you need in quick, concise doses. In addition, I've coined terms (here in italics) for many "New Girlisms" defined in a glossary at the back of the book.

What You Can Expect to Find Inside

So what will you find in this book? *New Girl on the Job* asks and answers tough questions like:

How can I learn not to take things so personally?

What's the best way to go about getting feedback so I don't get slammed at my year-end review?

How do I develop a thick skin?

How can I bounce back after I make a mistake?

How do I stand up to a difficult boss?

What are the professional boundaries with co-workers in social situations?

How do I handle my supervisor's sexual innuendos?

What do I do if I keep getting all the administrative tasks?

How do I assert myself when I feel like I'm being undervalued?

How do I self-promote without being obnoxious?

How can I negotiate my salary or get a raise?

What's the deal with mentors, and how can I find one?

How can I quit my job without burning bridges?

What do I do if I get fired?

You Need More Than a Nice Suit
and Black Pumps

In the November 2006 workplace issue of *Glamour* magazine, editor-in-chief Cindi Leive wrote, "When I started working eighteen years ago, pretty much the only advice I received was this, from a friend's mom: 'Buy black pumps.' So I strode into the working world with good shoes . . . and no clue about anything else."[1] Although Cindi started working two decades ago, her experience of preparing for the workplace is not much different from today; in fact, the majority of young women interviewed for *New Girl on the Job* said that buying a suit was the extent of their career preparation.

But we all know that in the highly competitive twenty-first-century workplace, you need resources beyond the salesperson at the department store. This is not to say that young women can't survive and flourish in their first couple of jobs without a book— many have and will continue to—but *New Girl on the Job* will empower young women intent on building a successful career. It's time to give the next generation of women moving through the workforce the potent combination of knowledge *and* tools to make their first steps on a career path positive ones, setting a precedent of success in these formative years.

1. *Glamour* magazine, November 2006, p. 30.

ACKNOWLEDGMENTS

New Girl on the Job would not have come to fruition without the voices of over 100 women, who shared their workplace experiences and insights with me. My deepest gratitude to all those I interviewed.

Thank you to Elisabeth Weed, my amazing agent at Weed Literary, who believed in this book in its infancy, and for her continued guidance and friendship throughout the process.

An enormous thank you to Alice Peck for teaching me how to make it "sing" and for having the big vision for *this* book from the very, very beginning.

A number of people provided instrumental help along the way. A huge debt of gratitude and the standing offer to put you all on a retainer one day to:

Dina Epstein, my dear friend and future business partner, for her feedback on an early draft. Jamie Kaufman, the jack of all trades, whose magic touch I don't know what I do without. Brienne Walsh for setting up the meeting that started it all and, thereby, putting the New Girls' Network in motion. Jayne Finst for all the material and support. Brooke MacDonald for being such an amazing guinea pig. Colleen Cary for modeling how to find a career not a job.

And finally, gratitude beyond measure to my editor, Danielle Chiotti, for her dedication to this book that never failed to come through with all of her keen editorial suggestions, and for being that rare hybrid: my editor and mentor.

NEW GIRL *on the* JOB

CHAPTER ONE

Making a Graceful Entrance
How to Find a Job You Don't Want to Quit

The beginning years in the workforce entail constant trial and error, and that often translates into a lot of turnover. Most young people take the first job that's offered to them, even if it's not the best match, because they feel like having a job is more important than having the right job. Sound familiar? Think about it: You probably don't know many people two years out of school who are in the same job they took right after graduation, and that number dwindles the more years you've been in the workforce. According to 2001 unpublished data from the Bureau of Labor Statistics, the median length of time workers in their early twenties stay in one job has shrunk by half since 1983—from 2.2 years then to 1.1 now.[1]

Like many young women starting out, Esther, 29, an architect in New York, says she was too eager to jump into her first job. After that experience she discovered the cardinal job-searching principle. "You really have to consider yourself a good enough product to sell. That way, you will look at a lot of places and not

---

1. Rick Marin, "Is This the Face of a Midlife Crisis?" *New York Times*, June 24, 2001.

1

just jump at the first offer. With my first job, I sort of jumped the gun and it wasn't the best experience. With my second job, which I'm a lot happier at, I came to visit the office and had them show me the project they were working on. Doing my due diligence made me a lot more confident about coming in on my first day, and ultimately happier and more productive at my job."

Making a Match

Finding the right job match is a lot easier said than done. The reality is that most people don't enjoy what they do. In a 2003 Career Builder survey, nearly one in four workers said they were dissatisfied with their job, a 20 percent increase over 2001. And six in ten workers said they planned to leave their job for other pursuits within two years.[2] But how do you even know where to start looking? To make the best match possible—and this sounds ridiculously obvious but is often overlooked—it helps to figure out what you are best at. The truism goes something like this: "Your learned skills augment your natural abilities." Figuring out what you are good at and matching those skills to a specific job are going to make finding a prospect and making a match a lot easier.

Steve Jobs, the founder and president of Apple Computer, Inc., said in his commencement address to Stanford's class of 2005, "I'm convinced that the only thing that kept me going was that I loved what I did. . . . Your work is going to fill a large part of your life, and the only way to be truly satisfied is to do what you believe is great work. If you haven't found it yet, keep looking.

2. "CareerBuilder.com Releases Comprehensive Report on Worker Trends and Plans to Change Jobs." November 17, 2003.

Don't settle. As with all matters of the heart, you'll know when you find it. And, like any great relationship, it just gets better and better as the years roll on."[3]

The essence of what Jobs says is important. If you don't find a job that in some capacity makes you tick, you will be miserable or, at the very least, less productive at work. Maybe finding the right match means you will have to start out as a cube monkey at some huge corporation, but then you should make sure it's a company where you could actually see yourself rising through the ranks. Or maybe it means that you get paid peanuts at a nonprofit, but you believe in the cause and that belief is what gets you up in the morning. Think of it this way—you'll work for ten thousand days of your life, and that's too many days to *not* enjoy what you do.

Bobbi Brown, founder and CEO of Bobbi Brown Cosmetics, is successful for a myriad of reasons, but she attributes it largely to the fact that she found a career that's constantly exciting to her— in other words, a job that gets her up in the morning and motivates her to keep going through all the daily sludge and drudge. Brown's advice to young women is that you've got to find the thing that tickles you.

If you are an accountant and you love fashion, perhaps try working in the accounting department of a fashion company. Marla Goonan, an executive career coach in San Diego, says this is critical to anyone starting out in the workforce. As a young woman, or young person for that matter, it's important to learn about yourself—what really fires you up and how you want to spend the rest of your life. Goonan says that the question you ask yourself is "What can I do and look back at ninety and feel good about?"

3. Steve Jobs, "You've gotta find what you love." *Stanford Report*, June 14, 2005. Commencement address.

Ask anyone who does something he or she loves and the person will tell you that it's a lot easier to be effective if you enjoy what you are doing and social science research proves it. Stephen Dubner and Steven Levitt, University of Chicago economists and best-selling authors of *Freakonomics,* explored this idea in a 2006 *New York Times* article:

> [Aders] Ericsson's research suggests . . . when it comes to choosing a life path, you should do what you love—because if you don't love it, you are unlikely to work hard enough to get very good. Most people naturally don't like to do things they aren't "good" at. So they often give up, telling themselves they simply don't possess the talent for math or skiing or the violin. But what they really lack is the desire to be good and to undertake the deliberate practice that would make them better.[4]

Lisa Witter, the general manager of Fenton Communications, says she put in years working for little pay at not-for-profits and knows firsthand how much doing what you love can drive success. "If you are staying late at work, or going to a networking event, you'll take more pride in what you do if you actually enjoy it. I would say that for the first five years, I was networking all the time. But I wasn't networking because I read somewhere that you have to network. I was doing it because I loved it." Witter now, at 32, is running her office.

Landing a job you'll love is really not all that abstract and mysterious. Like forming any partnership, taking a job is a leap of faith but, if you ask the right questions, you can often ascertain if it's going to be a good match, and it will feel like less of a leap.

---

4. Stephen J. Dubner and Steven D. Levitt, "A Star Is Made," *New York Times,* May 7, 2006.

Also, although it may seem counterintuitive, you can't just think about the job search process as a desperate quest for someone, or anyone, to hire you; you've got to think about it as if you are also making a hiring decision—that you are the chooser, not the chosen.

Judi Perkins, who has been a job search consultant for twenty-five years and is the founder of findtheperfectjob.com, says the people who are the most successful at finding a job they love realize they have the power of choice. "People who end up in jobs they really like aren't afraid to walk away from something that isn't what they want." Just because you've received a job offer doesn't mean it's the last job on earth. As women, we need to be particularly careful about falling into the "I'm just so lucky to have even *gotten* a job offer" mode of thinking. It's a better approach to think about getting the *right* job offer.

In terms of practical, applicable things you can do to scope out the situation and make as graceful an entrance as possible, Perkins says there is essential—and sometimes not so obvious information that everyone should find out on a job interview to determine whether or not it's a good match.[5]

1. Ask about job responsibilities. Job titles often provide no details about responsibilities, so be sure to ask the following questions during your interview:

- What are the priorities that will need to be addressed immediately in the position?

- Are you entering a newly created position?

5. Judi Perkins, "Five Questions to Always Ask on a Job Interview," Badbossology.com, May 1, 2006. www.badbossology.com/i10388-c171

- If not, was everything left running smoothly by your predecessor?

- Will you be picking up and continuing daily functions as normal, or be part of a new system within the company?

- Is there damage control that needs to be done?

- If so, is there a time line for the repair, and is it an achievable one considering your capabilities?

2. *Find out about the past.* Find out how long your predecessor had the job, why the person left, and if it was on good terms. This will help provide you with insight into some of the challenges of the position, and red-flag warnings as to internal problems in the corporation. In addition, scope out whether the company or department you are entering was recently restructured. A restructuring certainly doesn't mean anything bad (it happens all the time with the merging of companies) but it's part of the organizational landscape that you'll want to have information about. If you find out there was a recent restructuring, ask why and how that will impact the position you are interviewing for.

3. *Determine management style.* Succeeding in your new job is often dependent upon how you are managed. By asking your interviewer questions about him/herself, you'll be able to derive valuable information about the work environment you'll be entering into.

Before you go into the interview, think about how you are best managed. Do you respond more positively to a hands-on manager, or are you comfortable and more productive when your manager is hands off? If possible, during the interview, determine the management style of your potential boss.

- By asking: "What's your management style?" you'll be able to use context clues to determine if your potential boss is a micromanager or a hands-off manager.

- By asking: "How do you bring out the best in your employees?" you'll be able to determine whether your boss provides guidance to employees in need and if he/she will make a good mentor.

4. Assess the corporate culture. Perkins says it's important to ask questions that reveal the pervasive culture of the department, or company as a whole. Generally speaking, companies—or departments—tend to be made up of similar types of people that are in harmony with the company culture and philosophy, and it's smart to make sure you mesh well with that culture.

Therefore, it's perfectly acceptable (and will probably score you bonus points in the interview) to ask your employer which of the following personality types are a good fit for the company:

- Detail-oriented people

- Self-starting, big-picture thinkers

- People who work well in teams or committees

- People who require specific directions and stronger managerial supervision

Once you've gotten this information, you can assess how you'll fit in. According to Perkins, "An entrepreneurial person won't function well in a committee environment." By the same token, a person who needs a lot of structure might not function well in an entrepreneurial environment.

Bottom line: Do some soul-searching about the type of person you are and find a job that fits that. If possible, don't try to fit yourself into a work environment that doesn't match with your natural abilities.

5. *Look for growth opportunities.* Before accepting a job offer, you want to know if you are going to be stuck in assistant hell for the foreseeable future, or if it's possible to transition out of the position within a year or so. To find out, ask questions like:

- Is there a review after six months?

- How long was the previous person in the position
  before he/she got a promotion?

Another thing to pay attention to is whether both men and women have grown within the company. If the interviewer only gives you examples of men who have been promoted, you might want to think twice about taking a job there.

Red Flags

During the interview, be alert for potential problem areas about the job. For example, if your future boss comes across as a tyrant during your one-hour interview, just think what it would be like working for him/her forty-plus hours a week. Some other red flags to be on the lookout for:

- Employees are working with their heads down, there is minimal office banter, and the people you pass in the hallways look stressed or angry.

- A dearth of women in positions of power. Are most of the female employees in low-level, administrative roles?

- Your interviewer asks you personal questions, such as "Do you have a boyfriend?" "When do you plan on getting married?" "Do you plan to have children?"

- Your interviewer is taking calls, checking his/her BlackBerry, and paging his/her assistant, all while trying to conduct an interview. If this person can't make time for you now, it doesn't bode well for the attention you'll get once you are hired.

Career Coaches Aren't Just for People Who've Already Had Careers

While many assume that young people will just find their own way when it comes to a career, the reality is that it's much harder than that. With so many more options, high turnover rates, and fierce competition, your first few jobs can be, in a word, daunting, if not totally demoralizing. It's why we could all use a little extra help. And although we are supposed to get this "coaching" in college or graduate school, people who have visited their career-counseling centers often feel the way the January 2005 *Time* magazine article summed it up: "Most colleges are seriously out of step with the real world in getting students ready to become workers in the post college world."[6]

In this highly competitive job market, it's harder to get a career-building first job than it is getting into an Ivy League college. The 2004 National Association of Colleges and Employers annual survey says that the number of college graduates increased 12 percent a year in the last two years, but the entry-level job market remains 23 percent below the level for the year 2000. That's why this might be a good time to invest in some outside help. Profiled in a May 2006 *New York Times* article, D. A. Hayden and Michael Wilder, cofounders of Hayden-Wilder, a Boston firm whose clients consist primarily of newly minted college graduates, conducted in-depth interviews with fifty hiring executives at companies across the country in the summer of 2005, and were told by all of them that 80 to 85 percent of the job candidates they interviewed were poorly prepared.[7]

To prepare yourself, and give yourself the edge you'll need, Hayden recommends going beyond the cursory look at the company's Web site and really take your job search process to the next level. "If you are interviewing in the retail sector, for example, go look at the retail outlet, talk to customers, read analyst reports, read the chairman's letter." Essentially, you want to have value-added comments, observations, and perspectives. Even though

6. Lev Grossman, "Grow Up? Not So Fast," *Time* magazine, January 16, 2005.
7. Eilene Zimmerman, "Hoping to Get on the Fast Track, Students Turn to Career Coaches," *New York Times*, May 21, 2006.

these are entry-level jobs, you want to show that you've given the position some genuine thought. It's this approach, Hayden says, that lands 98 percent of her clients in career-track jobs.

Her advice to young women for achieving this goal is:

- **Find Your Focus**. This often takes a very serious examination of your natural skills, personality, and interests. Seeking outside help from a career coach can be useful in assessing these things. Hayden calls the people graduating *commencement castaways,* because they are left unguided.

- **Develop a Network**. This is a group of people you can call on to help you throughout this process. Start making a contact sheet of people you know, or would like to know, in your industry. Then start reaching out.

- **Do Your Homework**. You want to know everything you can about the organization. This means going beyond the Web site and mining every piece of material you can find. Taking it a step further, it means finding trustworthy secondary sources. Think of it as if you are doing the research to write a paper on the company or organization with which you are interviewing.

TAKEAWAYS

- Approach the job search process as if you're the person doing the hiring.

- Think about how your natural skills will augment your work.

- Find a job that makes you tick.

- Consider seeking career counseling, either through your school, or with a professional career counselor, to help you find your focus.

- Interview the company as much as they interview you in order to determine whether the job is a good fit.

- Do your due diligence, and make sure you have comments, observations, and insights beyond general knowledge about the company.

- Don't just think about finding "a job," think about finding a *career-track* job. Ask yourself, "How will this help me get where I want to be in twenty years?"

CHAPTER TWO

Becoming a Professional

There Are No "Do-Overs" When It Comes to Making a First Impression

The "New" You

Okay, you've researched to find the right job match, you've aced your interview, and you're in—you got the job. Now that you've scored the part, how do you act the part? It would be nice if, by just putting on your suit and pair of high heels, you could magically transform yourself into a professional, but the reality is that becoming a professional is a process that takes time, some good strategies, and a certain degree of faking it. But more on that in a minute.

Companies hire young people for a reason. They like the energy, enthusiasm, and fresh blood that newcomers bring to the workforce. In addition, young employees bring newer skills—particularly with regards to technology—and cost less in terms of benefits and salaries. However, it's a challenge to figure out how to strike a balance between acting like an über-professional and acting as if it is college orientation.

Plus, there are all sorts of facets to honing your professionalism that no one bothers to tell you about in college or graduate school or during your job interviews. For instance, how should you dress? Should you really have a work–life balance? Should you talk with your co-workers about your personal life? What is appropriate cubicle etiquette?

While "professionalism" differs from office to office, in all of these instances, it's smart to take a "better safe than sorry" approach. Until you learn the various ins and outs of your office, act, speak, and dress as professionally as possible.

Acting the Part: Am I Being Fake?

Mary, 22, a government employee in New York, recalled that during her first few months on the job, she was so overly formal with people that, as she put it, "I was just weird." Amber, 28, who now runs her own business in San Francisco, says that when she started working, she turned on her professionalism to such a degree that she felt as if she were much older than she actually was. She later toned it down and found a more balanced professional persona.

The key thing to remember is that it's best to set the tone from the beginning about how you want to be seen in the long term. This might mean moderating your personality to your office culture. For instance, if you are really outgoing, it might mean that you have to be a little more low key. And if you are really shy, it might mean that you have to work on being more social.

And if acting professional feels a little weird at first, it's because it is. Lisa Belkin, "Life's Work" columnist for the *New York Times*, writes that few of us ever bring our true selves to work. "We bring adapted and arranged versions, edited to fit the job. Our dress tends to reflect the rules of the workplace, written and not. We don't talk about our families nearly as often as we think about them. Our hobbies, our problems and our health are subjects generally left at home. We are someone else in the office: a flattened, incomplete, wan but professional version of ourselves."[1]

Lauren, 26, a consultant in New York, says she struggled with setting the right tone from the beginning. As a "gregarious" person, Lauren says, it was difficult adjusting to the concept that she couldn't exhibit these personality traits as much as she was used to in other parts of her life. "Coming in with a sense of humor and being bubbly really undermined my credibility. One of my managers even commented to me how much of a drastic change he saw in my ability to act 'professional' since the first day I walked into the office." Lauren found that once she got to know people a little better, she had more latitude to show her real self.

Sarah, 22, an assistant to the president of an event-planning company, also had to tone it down when she started working. "For me, toning it down meant that I couldn't blurt out every joke that occurred to me . . . I used to call my mom crying, telling her, 'I don't think I can be myself in a work environment. I'm too weird to be at work. I have to be half of who I am. This is horrible.'" Sarah slowly acclimated to only showing half of herself, and after six months on the job, she found that it got easier.

Just think of your first few months on a job the same as you would about adjusting to any new social situation. Things feel a

1. Lisa Belkin, "Life's Work: The Person Behind the Office Image," *New York Times*, November 6, 2005.

little odd or awkward at first and then as you find your footing, you gain confidence and become more comfortable.

Jill Herzig, executive editor of *Glamour* magazine, advises young women to think of their office persona as their absolute, best personality that is energetic and really positive. "It's exhausting to do this, I know. Your office persona shouldn't be something that is completely foreign. It is a version of yourself. It's you after your dream Starbucks cup of coffee. Instead, you have just got to keep that going—all day."

Speaking the Part: Because It's So Much More Than *What* You Say

As the actress and astute social observer Mae West once said, "It ain't what I say, it's the way that I say it." Though it may seem trivial at first glance, tone, delivery, and word choice really matter, particularly in a professional environment where so much is at stake. Deals, clients, and projects can go awry because of poor word choice and other nuanced language issues. Also, how you choose to express yourself both verbally and in writing will color how people perceive you, so start thinking about it sooner rather than later.

Judith Shapiro, president of Barnard College, was one of twelve women leaders who offered life lessons in *Newsweek* magazine in 2005. She expressed concern about the speech patterns of young women. "Women have to learn to speak with a pattern of quiet authority." Shapiro noted that, in addition to speaking in a nasal, rapid voice with rising intonations, young women often don't introduce themselves by their last name. It's a good point.

Who is going to remember you if you just say, "Hi, my name is Kate"? That's definitely not as powerful as "Hi, my name is Kate Franklin."

Another good tip comes from Phyllis Mindell's book, *A Woman's Guide to the Language of Success,* which was profiled in a 1996 *New York Times* article about the power language has to break the glass ceiling, in which she says that the *f* word—*feel*— is forbidden. Ms. Mindell advises readers to skip the "touchy-feely" syntax and head for the real subject. People who say "I (think/guess/feel) we need more time," are perceived as uncertain; people who say, "We need more time," or even "More time is needed" are not.[2]

Heather, 24, a software engineer in Los Angeles, says that whenever she has a problem with her boss, she writes what she characterizes as "long and emotional e-mails" that fall into the language traps mentioned above. To overcome this, Heather has a friend edit her e-mails to toughen up the language. Take a look at the before and after.

Before

After our meeting today, my concern is that it looks like everything will just work out, but I am still apprehensive. I have very strong feelings that things will change, or get postponed, and my schedule will be affected, considering that's how this has gone so far. So my worry at this moment is less based in fact, and more on a feeling or intuition of how things will go.

I appreciate the amount of trust and responsibility given to me on my first project, but I sometimes feel we are forgetting that

2. Deborah Stead, "Off the Shelf; Breaking the Glass Ceiling with the Power of Words," *New York Times,* January 7, 1996.

this is my first project and that overall it isn't going smoothly. Given these circumstances, and in order for the project to be completed successfully, I may need some help, or at least some support when I am asked why things are not complete already.

After

After clear indication from the team that production software is still incomplete, I have reassessed my project deliverables, their durations, and their need dates. A summary of this information is attached. I need your help in reviewing this schedule and conveying the information to the project team. I have been unable to successfully explain why software is not progressing to their satisfaction. I would also like to discuss possible strategies to ensure that from here on all of the software tasks are successfully completed on time. I will set up a meeting shortly to address these issues.

I will require support from others in software to obtain a comprehensive and solid design for the production software. This is my first project with the company, and I want to be certain that the budget for this project allows adequate time for the learning curve.

Guideposts for toughening it up

Take an inventory of your manner of speech in the office. Do you find yourself softening your sentences for fear of offending coworkers or sounding too demanding? Do you find yourself qualifying everything, instead of asking assertively for what you need? Do you phrase statements in the form of a question? Are you using the word "feel" interchangeably with "think"? The following list provides some fast fixes for touchy-feely language.

Instead of: *"I just feel that . . ."*
Try this: *"I think . . ."* or *"It has come to my attention that . . ."*

Instead of: *"I may need some help . . ."*
Try this: *"I will require help . . ."*

Instead of: *"I'm feeling like I might have trouble meeting my deadline."*
Try this: *"I have reassessed my project deliverables."*

Instead of: *"My feeling is less based on fact and more on intuition . . ."*
Try this: *"After assessing the facts . . ."*

Instead of: *"I sometimes feel like we are forgetting this is my first project . . ."*
Try this: *"This is my first project with the company, and the schedule and budget do not allow adequate time for the learning curve."*

In addition to learning to speak more directly, you should not be afraid to ask questions. Jennifer Baumgardner, author of *Manifesta: Young Women, Feminism, and the Future*, says that many women suffer from *fear of the dumb question*. "Women are less likely to expose themselves to asking a 'dumb' question because they don't want to be a burden." It's also, Baumgardner points out, because new employees are not trained to know what questions to ask right away. But how do you think really successful people got to the top? It certainly wasn't by sitting back and assuming all the information they needed to know would be magically imparted to them.

Judy Woodruff, senior corresondent for *The News Hour with*

Jim Lehrer, says she asked a lot of questions when she was starting out because, as is the case for many new hires, college didn't
teach her how to be a journalist. "I majored in political science at
Duke, but I didn't know how to be a political reporter. I was constantly asking questions." Woodruff says, too, that powerful people like to be asked questions, "It makes them feel good." Still,
it's tricky when you are new on any job to figure out how to get the
information you need without sounding helpless or apologetic.
Here are some traps you may fall into and some take-action pointers to help you turn your fear of asking questions into positive
results:

> **Trap:** *You try to complete an unfamiliar task on your
> own, because you are afraid to admit you don't know how
> to do it.*
> **Take action:** *Say to your boss, "I need to run through
> this with you once, because I want to make sure that I've
> got it down so I can do it correctly."*

> **Trap:** *"I'm really sorry to ask you this question, and I
> know I should know this, but . . ."*
> **Take action:** *"I was listening to your explanation
> earlier, and I just wanted to clarify a few things before I
> get started."*

Common questions about questions

Asking questions can be scary because you are, in effect,
acknowledging that you don't know something. Here are
some additional pointers about the logistics of asking questions:

Q: Who should I go to if I have a question about how to turn on my computer or access my voice mail?
A: Ask people on your level, not the head of your department or company. This is also an opportunity to introduce yourself to the company technology person, more commonly known as the IT person. Ask him/her if there are any manuals, tip sheets, or tutorials to get better acquainted with the technology at your office.

Q: Is there ever a situation where I should hold back on asking a question?
A: Yes—if you are at a client meeting or working with customers. Wait until you're alone with your co-workers. Don't blurt out a procedure-related question in the middle of a meeting!
  Also, if you have a question about something you think you "should" know, rather than asking the question when it pops into your head, take the time to research the question, and then come back and say, "I researched this and looked it up in X, Y, or Z, and I'm still having trouble coming up with an answer. Can you point me in the right direction?"

Q: Should I try to ask my questions when I first start the job? Will they think they hired the wrong person?
A: Yes, try to ask as many questions as you can during your first few weeks on the job. Colleen, 27, a government employee in Chicago, found that "if you wait a few months to start asking questions, you will start to get funny looks." You should take advantage of that golden

opportunity when you are new on the job and people
expect you to have questions.

Q: I asked a question, but the answer confused me even
more. Now what should I do?
A: There are two things you can do: (1) You can go back
and say, "I still need you to clarify a few things." (2)
Find someone else to ask. Remember, whatever you do,
just do something. It's better to take action than to ignore
the problem.

What Do You Mean "It's Not Personal"?

Probably one of the most important parts of becoming a professional is learning not to take things personally. Remember that
it's just business, so you've got to try to take the emotion out of
it. Amy Dorn Kopelan, former senior executive at ABC Television and president of Coach Me, Inc., a company that trains
women in the subtle skills and unwritten rules necessary for
leadership and advancement, captures the reality of the situation when she says, "It's harder for women to learn not to take
things personally. In fact, it's a bigger issue than anyone wants to
give credence to. If women learned more quickly to take things
less personally, they would be less afraid to raise their voices.
They would have more confidence to say what they wanted to say
and they would be braver." Kopelan went on to tell a story about
her husband's workplace: "Before a big meeting, my husband
said to one of the men who works for him, 'You aren't going to
wear those shoes to our meeting, are you? It doesn't make you

look the part.' The guy said, 'You are right. I don't know what I was thinking when I got dressed this morning.' " Later, when Kopelan's husband made the same type of comment to a female employee, the woman was offended and had a hard time moving on.

The concept of developing *a thick skin*—the ability to let things roll off your back and not take even the most hurtful comments personally—is an absolutely imperative element of professionalism. Dana, 28, a supervisor at a construction company in Los Angeles, says that she has learned that if you get offended at every little comment, you won't survive very long. Think about it this way: Getting offended takes a lot of time and energy you could be putting toward your work. Plus, your boss needs to feel that he/she can give you criticism, without the fear that you are going to be totally shattered by it. If your oversensitivity makes it difficult for your boss to give you an honest assessment of your work, you're going to have an uphill battle to a promotion.

Jill Herzig, executive editor of *Glamour* magazine, has worked for a variety of personality types during her fifteen years in the magazine business. She stresses that you can't take things personally, because ninety-nine out of one hundred times it's *not* personal. "It's often just the outgrowth of the pressures of the people around you that are letting off steam." Bosses, as Herzig points out, can be heedless about their manners. "Hopefully, you will be lucky enough not to work for a boss that wasn't raised in a barn, but there is that daily gruffness, the sharp voices, hollering your name in a loud, shrill way, instead of buzzing you on the intercom." You know how it is. And, if you aren't convinced yet not to take things personally, think of it this way: you never know the whole story. Early on in her career, Herzig worked with an established writer who was very difficult. The writer called her editor because she was upset about Herzig's edits. What Herzig didn't know at that time was this writer had just had her third child and, on top of it all, was trying to quit smoking. "I walked away from that meeting feeling like I had been criticized. I felt like I had been told my edits had been terrible. I was extremely upset about it and it really threw me off my game for a while. Slowly, though, I pieced it together that the writer had been under extreme stress and was in a pretty awful mood and was used to working with her old editor. Ideally, the senior editor would have explained this all to me." What happened to Herzig happens to everyone in the workplace, particularly New Girls. You don't know the *back story*—because you are new—and there could be a whole history that you are unaware of that impacts how situations play out. Her advice to young women is to say to yourself, "This is feeling sort of painful to me now, but there is more to this I don't know."

Developing a thick skin

Across the board, young women said that developing a thick skin was one of the biggest workplace challenges. Here are some tips on how to make it easier:

- Your boss and co-workers need to feel that they can give you feedback. Ideally, it should be in a constructive, helpful way, but we can't all be that lucky. Developing a thick skin is essential in the very likely event that you work for a boss who does not mince his/her words.

- Remind yourself there is always more to the situation (your boss might be having a rough time at home, or be under some other office pressure you don't know about), which affects the way he or she interacts with you.

- Things move so fast at an office that it's a waste of your time and productivity to get bent out of shape over every comment or criticism. Let it roll off your back and move on.

Dressing the Part

No matter what type of office environment you work in—casual, formal, or in between, you should always strive to display an appropriate level of professionalism in your clothing. Bobbi Brown, founder and CEO of Bobbi Brown Cosmetics, puts it bluntly about how young women dress for work. "A lot of girls have no clue how to present themselves. You have to open your eyes and look around and see what everyone else is wearing. I've seen too much cleavage, too many thongs, and definitely too many piercings. If you pierce something in college, please take it out."

Martha Burk, a political psychologist and women's equity expert, who led the effort to open the Augusta National Golf Club to women, has had young women work for her that she couldn't send on an outside assignment because they weren't dressed suitably. "If you aren't dressed appropriately and you send someone out to represent the organization, it destroys the organization's credibility."

To avoid professional dress code faux pas, here are some

answers to some of the most burning questions New Girls have about how to dress on the job:

What is business casual?

One of the most confusing—not to mention nebulous terms—concerning office dress codes is the marriage of business and casual. As a 2005 *Business Week* article succinctly summed it up, "It [business casual] was supposed to make life easier, but confusion reigns."[3] Although it's impossible to create a formulaic rule for dressing for business casual, you can't go wrong with the following:

- A pant suit

- An appropriate length skirt (below the knee) and a tailored sweater

- A button-down shirt with a skirt or pair of pants

- A wrap dress that isn't too tight or low cut

Can I wear flip-flops?

When Northwestern University's champion women's lacrosse team visited the White House and met with President Bush many people were more focused on the team's choice of footwear—flip-flops—than their national champion status. Suze Yalof Schwartz, executive fashion editor-at-large of *Glamour* magazine, was interviewed on CBS's *The Early Show* about this fashion choice.

3. Anne Field, "What Is Business Casual?" *Business Week*, June 9, 2005. www.businessweek.com/2000/00_44/b3705141.htm.

"They [flip-flops] are great for the beach. They're great for hanging out with your friends. But they're clearly unprofessional. They're not in fashion in the office, especially if you work in a corporate environment. And if you're going to the White House, cover up your toes."

Yalof Schwartz says it's fine to show some toe, just as long as the shoe is not plastic. "Toe is okay in the summer, as long as it's in a high-heeled strappy sandal."[4]

Can I wear tank tops?

According to Debra Lindquist, an image consultant who helped United Airlines create an image for their flight attendants, unless you are working at a job that involves a lot of manual labor, such as a shipping job, tanks tops are not appropriate: "My advice is that you want to dress to the highest common denominator. You always want to raise the bar rather than lower the bar. Sleeveless garments do not give you authority. Imagine if you saw a man in a sleeveless garment. They diminish the presence of a woman. If you already have the drawback of being young and inexperienced, you definitely don't want to diminish your appearance. You want more authority, not less."

Do I have to wear stockings?

This is slightly more complicated. The trend in shoes these days does not lend itself to hosiery. Lindquist says that if you go without hosiery, you are definitely projecting a less formal look. Her advice is that if you are wearing a typical business outfit, hosiery should be part of that outfit.

---

4. "Wearing Flip-Flops a No-No? Women Found It So After Wearing Them to the White House." *CBS News*. July 19, 2005.

What should I wear on casual Fridays?

The dress code for casual Fridays can be a minefield of confusion. In more conservative offices, casual Friday might mean no ties and khaki pants while in a more casual office, it might refer to blue jeans. To avoid a casual Friday mishap, ask a coworker what casual Friday in your office entails.

Even if your office casual Friday policy does permit jeans, keep it professional. Wear nice jeans and pair them with a button down, cardigan, or something that looks polished on top. However, if you are meeting with clients on a Friday, you might want to think twice about dressing casually, as *their* office might not have the same dress-down policy on Fridays.

Other things you might not have thought of when it comes to wardrobe

When you go shopping for work clothes, think Ann Taylor, not Forever 21. You want your clothes to look high quality. Along those same lines, invest in an iron, and budget your monthly expenses to include dry cleaning and tailoring. You don't want wrinkles, stains, and missing buttons to overshadow an otherwise professional looking outfit. It's just a fact that people will judge you on how you look. Lindquist says dressing is part of the halo effect. That is, if you observe one positive trait in someone (e.g., a person looked well groomed and put together), you will assign other positive traits to that person.

A final word about tight, revealing clothes: You never know who you are going to be doing business with. For instance, if you do a lot of business with overseas clients from more conservative countries or industries, they might be put off by low-rise pants and a tight top. That's why it is critical to be conscious of these things, especially when you are young. You can pretty safely assume that the following outfits do not bode well in any industry:

The Obvious Respect-Losers

- See-through shirts

- Belly shirts

- Skirts that you wouldn't want your grandparents to see you in

- Low-slung pants that reveal your underwear

- Anything that doesn't fit you properly, meaning that is either too tight or too loose

- Body piercings

- Low-cut, backless, spaghetti-strapped or cleavage-baring tops

- Clothes that you would lie around the house in on a Saturday afternoon

- Underwear worn as outerwear

- Any article of clothing that is wrinkled or visibly unclean

- Excess or noisy jewelry

- Strange hairdos

- Outfits that could be mistaken for a Halloween costume

- Extremely long nails

Overqualified and Underappreciated

It's hard to feel professional when you're earning less than what you were paid to be a camp counselor during the summer after your sophomore year in college. Take Anna, 23, an assistant editor at a fashion magazine in New York, who describes herself as a slave to the fashion world. She suffers from the common New Girl challenge—*the overqualified and underappreciated syndrome.* "I get twelve dollars an hour, no benefits, and no job security. If I worked at Best Buy, I would probably be a floor manager by now." People who are new to the workforce, in many cases, are paid the bare minimum and, at first, the accolades are few and far between.

Bevin, 26, a law student in North Carolina, has worked in a variety of jobs, doing everything from stand-up comedy to working as a doula. She realized quickly that you have to lower your expectations whenever you start in a new industry or field. "Personally, I was shocked at how mind-numbing the work was when I was working as a paralegal."

Elise, 29, now runs her own magazine in Chicago, but she also experienced the dashed expectations of starting out. "I got into the real world and expected all these things, but the reality was that I was living in a crappy apartment, had rats, and work was really hard." All of this can, understandably, take a toll on the ego.

Juliana Evans, a publicity manager at a major news network in Washington, D.C., has frequently observed the classic reaction to working at the entry level: "I'm too smart for this. I shouldn't be doing this." She reminds young women that there is nothing wrong with starting out as an assistant. "When you are starting out in your career, you have to pay your dues. I think in order to gain that access and have your opinion heard, you often have to do the mundane stuff and do it right. I'm not interested in promoting people unless I know I can count on you for the small stuff."

Evans is not the only person concerned about *Gen Y's sense of entitlement*. Bobbi Brown summed up what many other women at the top expressed about young women today. "I see a lot of young women thinking that a promotion is going to happen very quickly. You can't expect that in the first six months. I think you have to wait at least a year before you even ask for a promotion. You have to have the roots to grow strong."

Gail Evans, *New York Times* best-selling author, has watched this dynamic occur again and again. "Young women come in very well educated and smart and they work in a job for a year, and they think, 'I'm just as smart as the woman who works above me. I should have the same title as that person.' Young women judge their success by how fast they move up. It's very difficult for young women to understand that most organizations are very flat and there are a lot of people doing very similar things and the only thing that separates them is seniority. In most places you have to pay your dues. It's very hard. Young women think that they can do just as well as the lady down the hall. It takes a while. You rarely fly high as fast as you think you could."

So if paying your dues is inevitable, the career calculus should be doing so in a profession where you see a future. Sarah, 22, an assistant at an event planning firm, for example, doesn't think she'll spend the rest of her working life in the event-planning field, and therefore feels that her hours of thankless work are all for naught. Like many young women, she is disheartened that she worked hard through four years of college so that she could check a box that says, "Please include bread with our meal at this event." On the other hand, Anna puts in consecutive seventy-hour weeks at a fashion magazine where she's spending twelve hours a day organizing clothes and working most of the day in a dark closet, but can get herself up in the morning and put on a happy face, because she wants to be a fashion editor.

Wanting instant success can also be counterproductive to your career. Anna discovered quite quickly that her impatience—related to being a lowly assistant—led to a lot of unnecessary frustration. "You have to remember that you are twenty-three years old. Regardless of whether you think you are better than your boss, she probably has been doing it for fifteen years. Take a step back. You don't need to be a senior editor running the place, but it is so hard to be patient, particularly when you think you can do a better job. I'm always saying to myself, 'Did she really just pick that dress to go on that page. I could have picked something so much better,' but then I remember that she has years of experience on me."

Sue, 27, an employee at an architecture firm in New York, echoes this. "The biggest mistake I made coming into the workforce is not realizing that I have so much to learn. No one is a great architect overnight."

It's also important to keep in mind that while employers want to hire a go-getter with aspirations of moving way beyond entry level, it's equally important to present yourself as someone who is willing to take the steps to get there. Coming in with an attitude of entitlement is definitely a turnoff. For example, Amy Dorn Kopelan, now president of Coach Me, Inc., interviewed a young woman for an entry-level job at ABC television when she was a senior executive there, and turned the young woman down because Kopelan thought she reeked of entitlement. "The whole interview was about her. She would have been smarter, and more strategic, to come in and make it about me, and then six months later make it about her." Kopelan's experience with this young woman brings up a good point: It's a positive thing to believe you have the tools to accomplish big things—just don't let on that advancement is all you want. The trick is to feel deserving, but not to act it.

How to cope with the overqualified and underappreciated syndrome

Even though it's totally normal to feel overqualified and underappreciated, it's an ego blow that can be hard to adjust to. Here are some tips for how to soften the blow and set yourself up for success:

- Try to find a job where you see a true career trajectory so that the mundane work has a purpose.

- Remind yourself that entry level is about showing people you can do the small things so they'll feel confident giving you the bigger stuff.

- Don't take it as a knock on your ego. Everyone has to pay their dues.

- Entitlement is a turnoff to employers.

You Got the Job, Now Own It

With that said, no matter how lowly your position, you've got to own the fact that you got the job.

Gwenn Speak, vice president of Planit M, a modeling agency in New York, says lack of confidence is what stifles young women.

Don't let this lack of confidence undermine you in the workplace. If you think you don't deserve to have your job, or you aren't smart enough, or you don't know how to do the job, it will show in your work and the way you present yourself to others. You don't have to act as if you own the place; rather, project an aura of confidence that you know why they hired you.

Still not convinced you deserve your job? Try writing down a list of your skills and strengths, so you can remind yourself of all of the things your employer saw in you that made the company offer you the job in the first place.

It's totally normal to have some hesitation or lack of confidence about your abilities in your first few jobs. Whether you're working as a sous-chef, banker, newspaper reporter, or an assistant to the president of a large corporation, you're being taken seriously in a way you never have before by people who have at least a good decade or two of experience on you. It's no wonder you doubt yourself!

Jackie, 27, a child psychologist in Chicago, says she struggled with feeling like an imposter in her job. "I definitely had a hard time thinking of myself as 'a doctor.' I really doubted myself. One thing that helped me was to remember that you are never going to know everything, and that's okay. You totally just have to fake it a little. I couldn't believe that I was telling these people how to parent. Then again, though, I had gone to school for five years to learn how to do this."

Angela, 28, a junior associate of a law firm in New York, had to do a closing for a deal worth millions of dollars during the first two weeks on the job. "I had never done a closing before, so I just had to exude the confidence that I knew what I was doing."

Everyone starting out feels a little out of place, but that doesn't make you a fraud. It just makes you new to the workforce. But how do you deal with adjusting to a new job when your skills are still in development?

Martha Burk, political psychologist and women's equity expert, advises young women to own up to what they don't know how to do. "A manager would rather give you guidance than correct a mistake." Kathy Bonk, executive director and co-founder of the Communications Consortium Media Center, agrees and offers the reassurance that companies and organizations anticipate this learning curve: "So much of the time people are afraid that they don't know how to do anything. Most organizations understand that there is a transition for all new employees."

Office Etiquette

Another important area of your professional persona to develop is your office etiquette. This runs the gamut from the glaringly obvious (don't light scented candles) to more subtle social issues (how to offer your opinion in a meeting), and are well worth familiarizing yourself with to avoid workplace gaffes.

Cubicle etiquette

Cubicle etiquette is critical to being taken seriously as a professional. How you conduct yourself around your co-workers speaks volumes about your personality. If you work in a cubicle, here are some good things to keep in mind:

- *Don't take personal calls in your cube.* You don't want your officemates to know the intimate details of your life, or your best friend's life.

- *Practice volume control.* Find out what the technology policy is at your office before you start blaring music on your computer speakers or listening to your iPod.

- *Just as sound travels, so does scent.* Therefore be careful about what you eat in your cubicle. Subjecting your whole office to smelling your tuna salad all afternoon might not be the best way to socially ingratiate yourself. The same applies to scented candles—just because you love the fragrance of Jasmine Sunset, doesn't mean the guy at the desk next to yours will.

- *Don't decorate your desk the way you would your living room mantle.* That's not to say you can't have personal items on your desk, just take a cue from other employees at your office. If your co-workers do not have personal items on their desks, don't break out the picture frames and knickknacks. And if you do decide to put personal items on your desk, make sure they are tasteful desk ornaments. In other words, not pictures of you doing anything else that looks remotely unprofessional. It would be a shame to have inanimate objects on your desk make a bad impression.

Office etiquette outside the cubicles

But how should you conduct yourself in matters outside of your cubicle? There is perhaps nothing more important to cultivating your work persona and showing your boss that you're a valuable employee, than practicing good office etiquette. Here are some of the most common situations in which good office etiquette is indispensable:

Meeting important people (e.g., your clients) Master the art of a firm handshake and looking someone in the eye. Remember to introduce yourself by your first and your last name. Also, it's probably helpful to jog their memory. Say something along the lines of, "I'm Lucy Donovan, the account coordinator for the project."

Oh no! I've forgotten someone's name! No matter how careful you are, this will most likely happen to you. If it does, you can do one of two things:

1. If you absolutely must address the person, own up to the fact
you forgot. Say something like, "I am so sorry but I'm having a
brain freeze; please remind me of your name." And then don't forget it again.

2. If you are in a situation where you can fudge it for a while, hang
back and see if another co-worker fills it in for you.

Answering the phone The cardinal rule: no baby voices or
rapid-fire sentences. It's all about speaking clearly and slowly.

   If you're answering your desk phone for yourself, always use
your first and last name when you pick up. If you're answering the
phone for your boss, ask how he/she would like you to answer
his/her calls. For instance, should you use your boss's first and
last name, such as, "Hello, you've reached the office of Jane
Doe," or "Jane's office"? Should you mention something else in
your greeting, such as the name of your department? Do they want
you to say "Good morning," "Good afternoon"? Getting all these
details sorted out at the outset will help you avoid problems or
confusion, so you can present yourself as professionally as possible. This goes for setting up your office voice mail as well.

In a meeting *Always* bring a pad of paper and a pen for taking
notes, *always* make eye contact, *always* speak clearly, *never* chew
gum and don't bring in beverages until you establish that your
colleagues do. Don't interrupt your co-workers while they are
speaking. Instead, wait until they've finished their thought and
then find an appropriate lull in which to add your comments.

   If much of your job will be spent in meetings in which you'll
have to listen and add comments, it's smart to master the art of

active listening. Active listening is all about listening to another person in a way that improves mutual understanding and demonstrates that you are really hearing their point of view. To improve your active listening skills, it helps to restate the person's point. Say something along the lines of, "Adam made a really great point about how to increase efficiency with our Denver office, and I have another idea that I think we could implement as well."

If you have an opinion, by all means, speak up with your value-added comments, but tread carefully until you've had the chance to assess the projects you'll be working on and the roles of your co-workers in those projects. If you disagree with someone, be diplomatic by saying something like, "I hear what Jack is saying, but I was thinking about it like this." Another approach is do say something like, "As someone just jumping in at this stage of the project, it sounds to me that it might be helpful to consider X, Y, and Z . . ."

Social Etiquette

In the office, as in any situation where many people come together into one place, there is going to be some level of social interaction and chitchat. How you conduct yourself socially in the office is just as important as how you conduct yourself professionally. As tempting as it might be to gossip about your hot date, your family problems, or your big night out, you don't want to cross the line between personal and professional too early, if at all.

Nikki, 28, a fast-track ad executive in New York, said she talks to co-workers about her personal life but draws a line. "I talk to my colleagues about their significant others in a very surface way. However, I would never talk about how I got so drunk and threw up all over the bar. People who talk about that are perceived as the ones you don't want on your team." Plus, you want your co-workers to judge you by your performance at the office, not by your actions outside of work. If for whatever reason you seem disengaged or distracted on the job, your co-workers might interpret that it's because of the personal problem you couldn't stop talking about the week before.

A more subtle point about gracefully navigating social situations with co-workers is taking care not to come off as a know-it-all. Basically, you don't want to act like you are the vice president when you've only been in your position for a few months. Keep in mind that even if you take on more responsibility than your co-workers, it's not your job, or place, to become their boss.

Here are some quick examples of appropriate and inappropriate social talk:

It's okay to say: *"My boyfriend got on my nerves this morning."*
You probably don't want to say: *"I'm on the verge of a breakup with my boyfriend because we live with his parents and I want to move out."*

It's okay to say: *"I had a really fun night."*
You probably don't want to say: *"I can barely see this morning, I'm so hungover."*

It's okay to say: *"I'm having some family problems."*
You probably don't want to say: *"My parents are*

*going through a terrible divorce because my mom left my
dad for another woman."*

It's okay to say: *"I have a good grasp of the material,
and I'd be happy to help you with that project . . ."*
You probably don't want to say: *"This is so easy!
You really should know how to do it . . ."*

It's okay to say: *"I'd love the challenge of a project like
that . . ."*
You probably don't want to say: *"I should be put on
that project because I don't think the current team is
performing up to par."*

Using the Internet

The blanket rule regarding using the Internet at the office is:
Don't e-mail/IM/post/blog anything you wouldn't want your entire
office to see.

Surfing the web at work sounds harmless, right? Think again.
A federal law went into effect in November 2006 mandating that
U.S. companies keep track of all e-mails, instant messages, and
other electronic documents generated by their employees.[5] So
any Web browsing you wouldn't want your boss or the head of
your company to know about should not be done on office time.

Your work e-mail is company property. Many large corporations monitor their employees' e-mails, so obey the cardinal office
e-mail rule: Don't send personal e-mails from your work account.

5. Associated Press, "By the way, your boss may know you are reading this,"
December 1, 2006

Set up a separate account to do all your personal e-mailing from. It's an all too common mistake that's so easy to make with e-mail. You accidentally send a crude e-mail to your boss and not your friend because both of their e-mail addresses start "JO." But before you fire off personal e-mails from work, scope out your company's policy about checking personal e-mail on the clock. Some companies block most e-mail sites to avoid the problem altogether.

Instant messaging, while a convenient communication tool, can also pose problems at work. If your office uses it as a communication tool, make sure you use it as such and not as a way to chat with your friends all day. But if you do give in to the IM temptation, double check that it's not something your company or organization really frowns upon. As for the last technology frontier, if you have profiles on social networking sites such as MySpace, Facebook, or Friendster, give them a professional makeover during your job search. And if you didn't do it during a job search, do it immediately. It's risky business to have profile information, wall posting, and pictures that could in any way be seen as unprofessional. Anyone (read: your boss) can log on to these sites. In fact, employers screening candidates are increasingly turning to such Websites to learn more about potential and current employees.

Not Just a Catch Phrase:
You Need a Work–Life Balance

Becoming a professional means that other areas of your life are going to be reprioritized. This reprioritizing can spawn *workforce depression*. You know how it is as you mourn the loss of those carefree days when you actually had time to listen to music, have coffee with friends, and go to the gym. Young people in their twenties and thirties—be they male or female—are expected to work long and hard. So it's up to you to program a life back into your life.

Lindsey, 27, now a law student, says when she was working at a nonprofit in Washington, D.C., there was a snow day and everyone in the company was given the day off—except for her! She had to go into the office because she was the only one without a family to take care of. The lesson she learned is that, when it comes to cultivating a work–life balance, you have to draw the boundaries yourself. "No one is going to do it for you," she cautions.

Maggie, 24, who works in the health-care field in New York, discovered that her first work-related breakdown was triggered by having so little time for many of her interests and hobbies. "I used to listen to CDs, I used to Rollerblade, but I would come home so tired that I couldn't do any of those things. What really helped me get out of my funk was when I started feeding the interests and hobbies that had made me happy my whole life. If you don't do that, you will fall apart."

Programming a life back into your life is difficult because you are often working long hours. But you've got to keep yourself out of the *I'm-just-going-to-come-home-and-make-dinner-and-go-to-sleep-rut*. Whether that means that you read a book on the train, listen to music while you work, or carve out time to have dinner with your friends one night a week, you can't let your job completely take over your life. What starts to wear on you about being in the workforce is not the actual work. It's that you don't have time to do other things. You start to feel drained and depleted because you don't read books or watch movies anymore. Try to schedule even just a few of these activities back into your routine, and you'll start to feel better.

Lisa Witter, who runs a communications consulting firm, Fenton Communications, in New York, encourages young women to push their careers *and* their personal development. "If you don't push your personal development, you are going to be unhappy. It's your life. Go take a dance class. The people who do things like that are the ones that I respect the most. One of the young women who worked for me used to leave early once a week to take a dance class, and that only made me respect her more. The truth is, if people are able to develop themselves personally, they'll work harder for you professionally." So if you have interests, hobbies, or passions, make the effort to cultivate them, and you'll feel more satisfied—both in- and outside of work. Now, if only the rest of the workforce thought like that!

TAKEAWAYS

- Your office persona shouldn't be something that is completely foreign. It is a version of yourself that you tweak to fit the culture of your work environment.

- Be aware of the parts of your personality that you may need to tone up or down at the office.

- Speak the part, whether you're in your cubicle, in a staff meeting, or at a client function.

- Dress the part. Think Ann Taylor, not Forever 21, when building your office wardrobe.

- Don't be afraid to ask questions. Employers would rather help you get it right the first time than correct mistakes later.

- Develop a thick skin. Try to look at criticism as a way to improve yourself, and not a personal reflection on your work or personality.

- Don't use your company e-mail or Internet for personal correspondence.

- Be confident in your abilities! Own the fact that they hired *you*.

- Check your sense of entitlement at the door. It often takes more time than you think to move up the ladder.

- Make room in your life for a life. Work–life balance is extremely important.

CHAPTER THREE

X + Y

Navigating Female-Male Dynamics at the Office

Feeling comfortable and confident about navigating the social dynamics at the office is a critical component of succeeding at work with all co-workers—male and female alike. While this chapter focuses solely on interacting with the opposite sex, an in-depth discussion of female dynamics at work appears in chapter 7. Gender dynamics can be confusing to anyone, and especially to young women in the beginning stages of their career. Across the board, the dozens of young women interviewed for *New Girl on the Job* said that interacting with the opposite sex was often tricky, as there are no hard-and-fast rules beyond the umbrella terms of sexual harassment and gender discrimination.

Further complicating the issue is that young women today are accustomed to the egalitarian world of school, where the enrollment of men and women is generally equal, if not higher. The workplace, while slowly improving, is not quite as balanced. This chapter will give you practical advice about how to integrate into a male-dominated work environment; how to scope out the climate toward women at your office; how to draw boundaries (if necessary) with male co-workers; how to figure out which aspects of your femininity to bring to the office and which ones not to; what constitutes sexual harassment; and what to do if you become involved in an office romance.

Do a Background Check

Before you even think about taking any job, you should research the climate toward women at that company. Martha Burk, a political psychologist and women's equity expert, advises young women to do a *background check* to scope out how your potential employer treats its female employees. Burk says to look at the following: Are there a sufficient number of women in leadership positions? Have there been lawsuits mounted against the company for sexual harassment or discrimination? You can find out this type of information about a company through Internet sources, as well as by reaching out to other people who have worked or had experience with the organization. No one wants to come into a system that is stacked against her. To take your background check a step further, talk to women who actually work there. Ask them about their experience with advancement, work distribution, and other general gender dynamics at the office.

If possible, find someone who went to your college or graduate school, who either currently works or has worked for that company office. They are more likely to give you an honest assessment of the gender dynamics at your potential job. If you can't find somebody you know, reach out to another woman in

that same industry. If you want to dig even deeper, do a Google
or Lexis Nexis search about your potential employer, searching
with such keywords as "gender," "pay equity," and "advancement."

Help! I'm the Only Woman in an Office of Men!

In many male-dominated industries, such as finance, engineer-
ing, and law, coming to work can feel like you've entered a "no
girls allowed" clubhouse. Your male colleagues are rushing off to
play in their interbank lacrosse leagues, going out for beers, and
swapping tips on their fantasy baseball league, leaving you feeling slightly disoriented and left out.

But there are ways to acclimate yourself to male-dominated
workplaces or environments. Lee, 26, a financial analyst in Los
Angeles, learned to check the scores of the big game so she didn't
look completely clueless when the conversation turned to sports.
Angela, an associate in a law firm, says she tries not act overly
"girly": "For me, that means I use sports analogies. I talk the talk.
I don't whine, I don't gossip, and I don't complain about other
people."

Olivia, 24, a financial analyst in New York, knew that going
to work at an investment bank was the equivalent to walking
onto a football field. What was tough for her, she says, was looking at her office and not seeing any women higher up on the food
chain. "If you look at my industry, all the senior people are
male."

Olivia, however, has been extremely successful at integrating
herself into an all-male environment. She found that one of the

strategies that worked for her was acting as though she wasn't easily offended. "I didn't want the guys to tiptoe around me and alter
their conversations. These are people I spend fifteen to sixteen
hours a day with so I didn't want to have to *put on earmuffs* when
they were around. When you are working with all-guys, they want
to know that you can roll with the punches. I think if I had started
crying and showed that I was all emotional, it definitely would
have snowballed." Instead of getting offended, Olivia laughed
about their quest to make her cry. "That's when they really started
to respect me."

Working in a predominantly male environment is just like
working with any group of people who are different than you.
Meaning, you have to take some initiative to figure out how to
relate to them. That doesn't mean that you have to become like
them, just that if you have entered a male-dominated field,
you'll be best served professionally if you figure how to integrate.

The Generation Gap

Another common workplace situation that New Girls say they
came up against was a double whammy: the gender *and* age issue.
Statistics show that young women are increasingly entering work
environments where the age gap is, to say the least, noticeable.
The number of women between the ages of twenty-five and thirty-
four in managerial and professional jobs has increased 14.6 percent to five million in the five years from 1995 to 2000, according
to figures compiled by the Bureau of Labor Statistics. A 2000
Wall Street Journal article observed, "Everywhere, it seems,
young women are climbing off that bottom career rung and work-

ing alongside guys 20 and 30 years their senior."[1] This can be a culture shock for both parties. Older men, often for the first time, find themselves working alongside women young enough to be their daughters; and young women are reporting to male managers who probably rose through the ranks in a less egalitarian workplace. It's all part of the increasingly common *generation gap* in the workplace.

An important disclaimer here: Working with men from a different generation, although challenging to some young women, is not necessarily a bad thing. In fact, many young women found that men from a different generation were some of their biggest allies in the workplace. That said, some issues will surface nevertheless as a result of this generation gap.

Molly, 24, a third-year medical student in New York, says she constantly had to field comments from older, male doctors bent on discouraging her from going into certain fields. "I had one doctor in urology tell me that women should go into dermatology, radiology, or ophthalmology . . . He said I'm going to end up being a spinster if I don't." Caroline, 25, an assistant editor at a publishing house in New York, describes her fifty-year-old male boss as being somewhat chauvinistic. "A lot of the times he would go through the log of submissions and he would only give me novels that had female characters in them. Just because this novel has a woman in it, why does that mean I'm going to identify with it?"

But many times it's more than just fielding irritating comments, it's getting passed over for the top-notch assignments by

1. Ellen Joan Pollock. "Deportment Gap in Today's Workplace, Women Feel Freer to Be, Well, Women; Floppy Bow Ties Give Way to More-Alluring Attire; Sex Banter Has Its Place; Flirting—or Good Business?" *Wall Street Journal*, February 7, 2000.

your boss in favor of your male co-workers, by older men who aren't used to doling the cushy assignments to female underlings. Martha Burk, a political psychologist and women's equity expert, advises that if you find yourself in a situation where your male colleagues are getting all the best projects, you have to get documentation and present the evidence. She recommends saying something like, " 'Joe has gotten four of the five assignments given in the last month. If there is a criterion for the assignments that I don't have, I'd like to know what is.' I think a gentle, confrontational approach can work."

Burk cautions, however, that you don't want to keep hitting your head against a wall. "Women have to be realistic about what they are facing and what they can personally do to improve the situation."

However, you may find yourself in a situation in which the issue is less about missing out on the plum assignments and more about fielding inappropriate, off-color sexual comments— a situation that is inevitably awkward and uncomfortable when it's coming from an older, male boss. When senior *News Hour* correspondent Judy Woodruff got her first job out of college, the man who hired her said, "How could I not hire someone with legs like yours?" As a new hire, Woodruff didn't make an issue out of it, but she says that if he had continued to make comments like that she would not have put up with it. That experience taught her that you have to constantly be aware and draw boundaries. For young women this is hard, particularly when the advances are from your boss or any other influential person in your company. If you experience such problems, it's time to reach out to more senior women who have probably been in your same situation, and maybe even with the same guy. A young woman sought Woodruff's advice when she was propositioned by a male superior. "She came to me because this was a guy in a very powerful position and she didn't know what to do. I told her to tell him that she had just gotten engaged to her boyfriend, and that her boyfriend didn't want her going out with other guys. That worked to deflect it."

Some other good responses to deal with the more pesky comments:

- "I don't think your wife (or girlfriend) would want to hear you saying that to me."

- "I don't think that is an appropriate discussion for the office."

- Make it a point to mention that you are the same age as his daughter, niece, or granddaughter. There's nothing like putting it in the family context to get the conversation back to a professional topic.

Sexual Harassment: The Lowdown

Corroborating what so many young women said they experienced in the workplace are statistics that indicate that sexual harrassment is still rampant in many offices. In 2005, according to the Equal Employment Opportunity Commission, women filed 86 percent of sexual harassment claims.[2] It's also something that,

2. Statistics compiled by the Equal Employment Opportunity Commission: Women filed 86 percent of all sexual harassment charges in 2005. www.eeoc.gov/stats/ harass.html

unfortunately, appears to disproportionately affect young women. Boston lawyer Liz Rodgers, a partner at Rodgers, Power & Schwartz, commented in a 2004 *Boston Globe* article that young women are often the focus of unwanted conduct because they seem vulnerable and gullible.[3]

There is a huge caveat to be aware of here—part of working with the opposite sex is the fun, playful, banter that naturally occurs with people that you end up spending the majority of your time with. Offensive jokes are told, and you've probably fielded a question or two about your personal and sex life, which is all fine, as long as it doesn't jeopardize anything professionally for you. Meaning, whatever behavior you are engaging in is not tarnishing your reputation in a way that could hinder a promotion, ignite harmful office gossip, or put you in a compromising position with a co-worker or boss.

But let's talk about those workplace situations that do cross the line. David Swink, president of Strategic Interactions, an organizational consulting firm, has run hundreds of workshops on sexual harassment. He says that company policies are often stricter than the law when it comes to sexual harassment. According to Swink, "For something to be sexual harassment, someone has to feel that it is unwelcomed." If at all possible, he advises that young women should first try to have direct, open, and honest communication with the person they feel is harassing them. One useful way to start this inevitably awkward conversation is: "I know it's not your intention, but I felt violated." Swink also stresses, though, that you have every right to say no to any advance.

The statistics on the repercussions of sexual harassment are

3. Diane E. Lewis, "Sexual harassment still dark cloud in workplace," *Boston Globe*, October 31, 2004.

staggering. According to a 1986 study in the *Administrative Science Quarterly*, women are nine times more likely than men to quit their jobs, five times more likely to transfer, and three times more likely to lose their jobs because of harassment. So, if a situation with a male co-worker leads you to contemplate quitting your job or transferring divisions, or is preventing you from operating at full throttle, it's probably time to seek an intervention. Find out, too, if other women are feeling harassed by that same person or workplace atmosphere. Strength in numbers is always helpful. It's also important to know your company or organization's specific policy on sexual harassment. Every business has a different policy. You can get this information from Human Resources or in the employee manual. Also, you want to be familiar with your company's policy and procedure on reporting sexual harassment. For instance, do you have to have documentation in the form of e-mails, phone conversation, or other evidence? Figure all that stuff out before you file the official report. Martha Langelan, Hugh Garner, and Catherine MacKinnon's book *Back Off! How to Confront and Stop Sexual Harassment and Harassers*, states any of the following unwanted behavior may constitute sexual harassment.[4]

- Leering

- Wolf whistles

- Discussion of one's partner's sexual inadequacies

4. Martha J. Langelan, Hugh Garner, and Catharine A. MacKinnon, *Back Off: How to Confront and Stop Sexual Harassment and Harassers* New York: Fireside Press, 1993, p. 25.

- Sexual innuendo

- Comments about women's bodies

- "Accidentally" brushing of sexual parts of the body

- Lewd and threatening letters

- Tales of sexual exploitation

- Graphic descriptions of pornography

- Pressure for dates

- Sexually explicit gestures

- Unwelcome touching and hugging

- Sexual sneak attacks (e.g., grabbing breasts or buttocks)

- Sabotaging of women's work

- Sexist and insulting graffiti

- Demands such as, "Hey, baby, give me a smile"

- Inappropriate invitations (e.g., hot tub)

- Sexist jokes and cartoons

- Hostile put-downs of women

- Exaggerated, mocking "courtesy"

- Public humiliation

- Obscene phone calls

- Displays of pornography in the workplace

- Insistance that workers wear revealing clothes

- Inappropriate gifts (e.g., lingerie)

- Hooting, sucking, lip-smacking, and animal noises

- Pressing or rubbing up against the victim

- Sexual assault

- Solicitation of sexual services

- Stalking

- Aggressive invasion of personal space

How Much "X" Should I Bring to Work?

Enough about the downside about being a woman in the workplace. It's certainly not all about being the target of offensive comments and warding off predators. There's a huge upside to being women and, lucky for us, the twenty-first-century workplace seems to be embracing, albeit slowly, what women bring to the boardroom.

It can be a slippery slope—and one well worth thinking about how to navigate. The front page of the *Wall Street Journal* on February 7, 2000, read, "In Today's Workplace Women Feel Freer to Be, Well, Women. Floppy Bow Ties Give Way to More-Alluring Attire; Sex Banter Has Its Place. Flirting—or Good Business?" The article explored how young women today are less inhibited about using their personality to get ahead professionally.[5] So the question remains: How much of your female self should you bring to the workplace?

Angela, a lawyer, says that sometimes she plays the "innocent young woman" role. "Particularly when I'm negotiating, it will lower the other lawyer's defenses. In some situations, you have to give a false sense of security when you are dealing with people in any sort of adversarial role. You let them talk themselves into a corner."

The empowering part is that young women feel like they can incorporate their femininity into their office persona. It's an ability Chelsey Owen, cofounder of the Summit Employer Group, an online human resources firm, coined the term *integration* for, the concept that young women want to integrate all aspects of their personalities into the workplace. Integration is really about learning how to use your personality to your advantage. Women and

5. Pollock, "Deportment Gap in Today's Workplace."

men each bring a distinct skill set to the table. Women, for instance, have been lauded as more effective consensus builders, savvier communicators, better listeners, and more adept at reading subtle social cues—all skills that can give them an enormous amount of leverage at the office.

Although using your personality to your advantage is great, it's crucial to keep in mind exactly which aspects of your femininity you should integrate into the workplace. Allowing your natural personality to shine through can be viewed as an asset, but be careful about not slipping too much flirtation or sexuality into your actions. As anyone who has made it to the top will tell you, relying on your sexuality at work is not a good, or long-term, strategy. Oprah Winfrey certainly didn't get where she is today because she used her sexuality, and she's not the only one.

Patricia Ireland, former president of the National Organization for Women, calls flirting a "short-term strategy." "In this culture, being attractive means being young. And you will be conventionally attractive—that is, your flirtiness will be considered interesting and intriguing, rather than pathetic—as long as you are still young and conventionally attractive."[6]

Anne Northup, a former Republican congresswoman from Kentucky, was quoted in an interview in the wake of the Monica Lewinsky scandal as saying, "Women get the feeling that their careers depend on being coy and seductive rather than working hard and bringing their talents to the workplace."[7]

Flirting may also have larger repercussions. In a 2005 study, researchers at Tulane University measured whether sexy dressing and sexual behavior negatively impacted the careers of women—and the researchers found that they did. Women who

6. Ibid.
7. Jonathan Broder, "The Silence Is Deafening," Salon.com, March 31, 1998.

send flirtatious e-mail, wear short skirts, or massage a man's shoulders at work win fewer pay raises and promotions. In a somewhat alarming finding, 49 percent of 164 female MBA graduates said in a survey that they have tried to advance in their careers by sometimes engaging in at least one of ten sexual behaviors. Women who claimed they had never engaged in sexual behavior had earned an average of three promotions. Those who stated that they had engaged in flirting and other overt behavior had only earned two promotions.[8] Keep that study in mind the next time you think about integrating flirtation into the workplace.

Office Romance

From television to real life, everyone loves the intrigue of an office romance. Chances are, you know a lot of people who have had everything from one-night stands to long-term relationships at the office. How boring would *Grey's Anatomy* be without the romance between Dr. Cristina Yang and Dr. Preston Burke?

But TV and real life are two very different things, so please proceed with caution. A *New York Times* article that came out in the post-Lewinsky media storm made a very important point that while a romantic relationship with one of your co-workers of equal power may be acceptable, a relationship between two people with unequal power can become complicated: "Labor lawyers, human resource managers and consultants like Holly Culhane agree: sex and romance between co-workers may be

8. Del Jones, "Study Says Flirtatious Women Get Fewer Raises, Promotions," *USA Today*, August 4, 2005.

acceptable, but almost never between people of unequal power. Policies at I.B.M., General Motors and other leading companies reflect this thinking. And by 'unequal power' they don't mean simply the C.E.O. and his secretary. In the new economy, among educated professionals and all those managers and would-be managers who work so closely together in teams and late into the night, and often on the road after wine-besotted expense-account dinners . . . you get the picture."[9]

In a workplace situation, wouldn't you rather be evaluated by your boss, not your boyfriend? Plus, dating your boss has a lot of potential to tarnish your reputation. Finally, romantic involvement with any co-worker—especially your boss—brings a layer of emotion to work that will make it more difficult for you to do your job. You may begin taking normal workplace feedback more personally than you did previously. It can start with something simple, such as wondering why he used a terse tone when he asked you to look over the report and spiral downward from there.

Obviously, office romances are tricky situations for which there are no blanket solutions. Many advocate the "Don't get your honey where you get your money" policy, while others point to meaningful long-term relationships at the office. According to a survey of employees released in February 2005 by career publisher Vault, 58 percent of respondents said they have been involved with a co-worker and 22 percent said they met their spouse or significant other at work.[10]

So if you are thinking about becoming involved with a co-worker, consider the following:

9. Philip Weiss, "Don't Even Think About It (The Cupid Cops Are Watching)." *New York Times,* May 3, 1998.
10. Sarah Max, "Love on the Company Clock." CNNMoney.com, February 11, 2005.

- Does your company have an intraoffice romance policy? If it does, what is it? If there is a firm no-dating policy, are you still going to proceed? What are the repercussions either way?

- If you're in an office relationship, how should you act at the office? How much contact should you have during the day? How are you going to act at the office if you break up?

- Should you tell your boss or other people on your team about your relationship?

David Swink advises young women who find themselves in office romances to beware of doing a lot of public flirting and a lot of touching. No one likes public displays of affection (PDA) and people *really* don't like it at the office. He also advises having a *contingency plan* with the person you are dating in the event that the relationship doesn't work out.

As regards disclosure of these relationships, Swink suggests that if one person reports to another, it would be smart to tell a superior and maybe even Human Resources, to avoid problems later. If you are working on a team or project, your co-workers are probably going to pick up on the romance vibes anyway, and it takes a lot of energy to keep that kind of secret quiet. It could also undermine trust on the team. Swink's other advice is to keep the norms of the organization in mind. "In some organizations, a lot of people date co-workers. In other organizations, it is more of an unspoken taboo."

No matter what field you work in or what rung on the ladder

you are on, there will be a point in your career in which you are faced with some sort of clashing gender dynamics at work. Knowing how to navigate male/female dynamics will help you form positive relationships with your male co-workers and and avoid falling into the traps that have stymied women in the past.

TAKEAWAYS

- Do a background check on your potential employer to assess the climate toward women at the company.

- If work distribution appears to be unequally slanted toward your male co-workers, address gender inequities by presenting your boss with a concrete list of facts and examples.

- If you find yourself in a male-dominated environment, figure out ways to socially ingratiate yourself, whether it's reading the sports page *once* a week or going out for beers with your co-workers. It's well worth it professionally to try to have some social connection to them.

- If you find yourself in a gender-biased situation you don't know how to handle, reach out to other, senior women at the company—they've probably been there.

- Become well versed in your company's formal sexual harassment policy, so you know what does—and doesn't—cross the line.

- Think about which parts of your personality you want to integrate into the workplace. Remember, flirting is a short-term strategy that has an impact on your paycheck.

- Before you get romantically involved with a co-worker, find out your company or organization's policy about office dating. If you do decide to proceed with a relationship, have a conversation with that person about how you'll act if you break up.

CHAPTER FOUR

Bad Bosses

What to Do When Your Direct Report Treats You Like an Enemy, a Lover, or Anything in Between

A challenging boss is a ubiquitous part of any workplace experience. We've all had one—the kind of boss that makes you want to hide under your desk at the sound of his (or her) voice. If you don't know how to deal with them, bad bosses can erode your self-confidence, which can prevent you from doing your job to the best of your ability. A February 2006 *Wall Street Journal* article, "Dealing with Bad Bosses," quoted Barbara Moses, a social psychologist and president of BBM Human Resource Consultants, about the case of an employee who was so angry at his boss that he systematically cut the boss's jacket when it was hanging in the closet.[1] Let's try to avoid a situation like that one by giving you tools and strategies to deal with a bad boss that don't involve scissors.

Dena, 27, an attorney in Washington, D.C., says that the most important workplace skill she has learned is dealing with bad

---

1. Andrea Coombes, "Dealing with Bad Bosses," *Wall Street Journal*, February 26, 2006.

bosses. "I think as young women, we often don't want to deal with conflict. All of my friends say they were shocked by how difficult relationships with bosses could be. I certainly took my inter-actions with my bad boss as a knock on my capabilities. I was always thinking there was something that I could be doing differ-ently, or that maybe I needed to be more deferential. I found myself starting to avoid people."

This chapter outlines how to deal with a variety of bosses—from the boss whose behavior runs hot and cold, to the boss who won't give you a straight answer, the boss who bullies, the boss who hits on you, and the boss who silently sabotages. Although it's impossible to change your boss, having some quick tricks (i.e., tools and strategies) at the ready will empower you against any bad-boss situations you may encounter.

Warning: Bad Bosses Are Pervasive

Statistics reveal that bad bosses exist in offices throughout Amer-ica. Richard S. Wellins, a senior vice president at Development Dimensions International, estimates that one in ten leaders cross the line from managing to bullying their employees.[2] Compound-ing the problem is often a lack of resources to deal with these bad bosses, which underscores the importance to young women of developing defensive skills early on. The bigger picture, too, is that you might have dreamt of a career as a scientist all your life, trained for it, and then find yourself thwarted by a bad boss. John Hoover, the author of *How to Work for an Idiot: Survive and Thrive . . . Without Killing Your Boss*, confirms through research

2. Lisa Belkin, "Life's Work: Working for a Boss Who Bullies," *New York Times*, May 8, 2005.

what so many of us at the bottom of the totem poll already know: People cite bad bosses as the number-one reason they leave jobs.[3]

Today, one in three American workers say they've experienced two harmful acts at work weekly in the last months, including everything from being expected to handle an unmanageable workload to yelling, shoving, and even being the butt of practical jokes.[4] In addition, bad bosses is a problem that's almost three times more likely to affect women. Psychologist Michael H. Harrison, Ph.D., of Harrison Psychological Associates notes that a survey of nine thousand federal employees showed that 42 percent of female but only 15 percent of male employees reported being harassed during a two-year period (with a cost of more than $180 million in lost productivity).[5]

If you're stuck with a bad boss, a key point to keep in mind is that they are not necessarily bad people. It just might be that they lack the management skills to oversee new hires. The reality is that a lot of people rise in the ranks of a company not because they know how to manage people, but because they've excelled in other areas. And once they are promoted into management position, they are given very little management training. For example, many large corporations offer a mere three-hour training seminar on how to deal with your underlings—talk about a crash course! With such a lack of consistent, comprehensive training, it's important that you know how to deal with managers who don't get this training—it's really a vicious cycle.

3. Claudia H. Deutsch, "At Lunch with—John Hoover: Idiots, and the People Who Work for Them," *New York Times*, January 4, 2004.
4. Dawn Sagario, "Survey Finds Bullying Common at Work; Researchers Found That More Americans Than Europeans Reported Abuse," *Des Moines Register*, July 26, 2004.
5. Liz Urbanski Farrell, "Bullies in Business Besmirching the Bottom Line" *Business First of Buffalo* (NY), February 11, 2002. www.bullybusters.org/press/bizfirst021102.html.

Is It Me? Or Is It Them?

Dealing with a bad boss often feels like a no-win situation, and it's not uncommon to begin doubting yourself: *Am I taking this too personally? Or is my boss just being a big jerk?* What is so confusing about bad bosses is that unless they violate the "big two" (sexual harassment and discrimination), it is often difficult to take formal measures to address the problem. While a boss who yells at you, bullies you, sabotages you, or doesn't give you adequate support probably isn't doing his/her job as well as he/she could, none of these incidents fits precisely within the parameters of something that could be formally reported. As *New York Times* "Life's Work" columnist Lisa Belkin points out (quoted in an August 2005 *Wall Street Journal* "Marketwatch" article), "Bullying is technically not against the law. Statutes prohibit sexual harassment, racial harassment and physical assault at work, but unless a rampaging boss boils over into one of those areas, he has, in a legal sense, done nothing wrong."[6]

In your first couple of years in the workforce, it's often unclear whether you're dealing with a problem of your own making or if your boss is the one out of line. Unfortunately, there are no canonized rules on what is considered "inappropriate office behavior." Kathy Bonk, co-founder of the Communications Consortium Media Center, sets a gold standard for how bosses *should* treat their employees. "I think it is totally unacceptable to be in a workplace where people are yelling at you and where tempers get in the way. Abuse is not a way to run an organization. Respect is a critical value in any workforce. Once the respect starts to break down, things begin to spiral." Bonk says

6. Marshall Loeb, "No Shortage of Poor Management: How to Deal with a Bad Boss." www.careerjournal.com/myc/survive/20050826-loeb.html

that if she snaps at an employee, she'll apologize. Now, if we could all be so lucky.

Bad Bosses: More Than Just a Tic

Dealing with a difficult boss is more than just an unpleasant part of your day. According to studies, job stress is far and away the leading source of stress for American adults. In fact, the National Safety Council estimates that one million employees are absent on any average workday because of stress-related problems.[7] In light of all of this, it's important for young women to have an approach for dealing with bad managers.

The Criticizer
The Criticizer is a real confidence killer. It seems like, no matter how well or how poorly you do something, you get the same result: criticism. Although constructive criticism is helpful, constantly being told that what you are doing is subpar can really take a toll on your work productivity. Take Arya, 24, a political consultant in New York, who had worked for a Criticizer. "He waited for me to make a mistake so he could pounce. Among other things, he often told me that I was 'slipping' every time I missed so much as a comma on an interoffice memo." At first, she took his comments personally because "my conscientiousness has been such a strong suit in everything that I've done." Ultimately, Arya became run down by the constant criticism, and she quit. But that certainly doesn't have to be the outcome.

7. Gary Namie and Ruth Namie, Ph.D. *The Bully at Work: What You Can Do to Stop the Hurt and Reclaim Your Dignity on the Job.* Naperville, IL: Sourcebooks, 2003, p. 59.

Coping with the Criticizer. No matter how critical the Criticizer gets, there are things you can do to counter these actions and protect yourself:

Wait for a time when you are calm, cool, and collected, and then confront the Criticizer. A stream of constant criticism from your direct report can be stressful enough to make you want to lash out. But that's definitely not the most effective way to handle the situation.

When Abigail, 22, a first-year employee at a recruiting firm in Chicago, couldn't take the nitpicking from her boss anymore, she nearly blew up one day. "Instead, I decided to wait for a time when I wasn't brewing with so many emotions so she would take me seriously and not just as some overemotional girl. I'm glad I made that decision because it put me in a better, more authoritative position when I did confront her."

Make use of analogies. When, or if, you decide to approach the Criticizer, try framing the situation in terms of how it is impacting your work. You can say something along the lines of, "I wanted to talk to you about how I could do a better job, and it's difficult to deliver a hundred percent when I'm being constantly criticized."

If you're looking for a more subtle approach, analogies can be very effective. They make the situation seem less personal and can give your boss another context in which to think about the situation. Say something along the lines of, "A coach encourages his players, or at least tempers his negative and positive feedback. 'Amy,' you are sort of like a coach right now, and I'm your player. If you constantly criticize your players, they will lose confidence, and that will ultimately impact their performance on the field. Is that what you want?" In a best-case scenario, it will empower "Amy" to take on more of that "coaching" role.

If all else fails, remove yourself from the situation. No matter how much of an effort you make to improve the situation, there may be times when your boss just doesn't respond positively. At this point, it's up to you to make a decision between remaining in a job situation that could be damaging to your career or moving on to a (hopefully) more positive environment.

Lauren, a consultant, made many attempts to talk to her boss about her constant criticism and nitpicking. "Every time I confronted her about how she was managing me, her response was that I needed to just step it up and do this, this, and this. I couldn't learn, and operate effectively with someone constantly criticizing me. I explained to her that I would be better motivated by someone who was positive, but that just didn't sink in with her." Finally, Lauren asked to be removed from her assignment altogether. "It was a bold move on my part to be taken off the project, particularly because I was so new on the job, but I ended up getting assigned to a better project."

The Micromanager

The Micromanager makes you feel as if you're being stalked, and that's probably because you are, to some degree. The Micromanager watches everything you do. And as anyone knows who has worked for a Micromanager, it's hard to get work done (and done well) when it feels as if a vulture is sitting over your shoulder.

Managing the Micromanager. If the Micromanager in your office is making you miserable, try some of these tips:

Remember: It's not you, it's him. Shaun Belding, author of *Winning with the Boss from Hell*, says that micromanaging is very often a personality trait of your boss, and not a reflection on the quality of your work. A Micromanager at the office is most likely a micromanager elsewhere in life.

Let the Micromanager think he/she has control. Since micromanaging is more about control than anything else, Belding advises that the quickest path to getting your job done efficiently is letting your boss *think* he/she is in control. So, use less important situations to your advantage, and ask things like, "Would you like me to plug the shredder on the far wall, or would you like to plug it in by the door?" The bottom line, Belding says, is that you have to give your boss the illusion that he/she is in control.

Take a preventive approach. Don't give the Micromanager any more ammunition for peeping over your shoulder than necessary—double-check your spelling, grammar, and formatting on memos. Recheck the sources on your research. Whatever your job is, make sure that your work is up to par to avoid run-ins.

The Slave Driver

Although you are flattered that your boss thinks so highly of you that he/she has faith in you to do the impossible, the constant bombardment of work can actually get in the way of your job. As Susan, 25, an assistant producer at a major TV station in Los Angeles, puts it, "The Slave Driver will ask you to do the impossible, and all while calling you and e-mailing you simultaneously to ask you to do more things." In addition, the time frame that the work is expected to be done in is often unreasonable.

Taming the Slave Driver. The key to dealing with the Slave Driver is not to make the issue about how the enormous workload is affecting you personally. For example, you don't want to say, "I missed my grandfather's ninetieth birthday and my college reunion because of all the work you are piling on."

Instead, make it about how his/her management style is having a bottom-line effect.

Make it clear that the workload is impacting your ability to do your job. A heavy workload can quickly snowball into an unmanageable one. To stop this before it starts, you should talk to your boss.

Try approaching your boss with a statement in this way: "It's difficult for me to deliver a good product with such an unrealistic timeframe to complete my work. Can we reassess the time line so I can give you the best product possible?"

Whitney, 25, says when she worked as a paralegal at a big New York law firm, people would ask her to do unreasonable things all the time. "I learned quickly that you tell them that it is unreasonable, or you are clear about how much time a task like that will take to complete."

Turn the tables. As long as you let the Slave Driver get away with it, he/she will continue his/her ways. Ashley, 27, an account coordinator at a public relations firm in Chicago, discovered a great technique for confronting her boss, who kept piling huge amounts of work on her. She asked, "What do you think is the most effective way to manage a heavy workload?" Ashley says it opened up a conversation with her boss about work delegation and how to come up with a system that was more productive for both of them.

The Humiliator

Your first question about the Humiliator might be, "Is this a joke?" because his/her heedless way of yelling at you in public, in front of large groups of people, is just plain bad manners. But it goes deeper than that, because the Humiliator is the kind of boss that thinks public embarrassment is an effective management style.

Breaking the Humiliator's habits. With the Humiliator, it's all about setting boundaries. To do this, try some of these tactics:

Be as direct as possible. This is not a situation in which to beat around the bush. When dealing with the less-than-polite actions of the Humiliator, be as to-the-point as possible. Say something like, "It reflects poorly on our team if I feel undermined and devalued. Can we arrange to sit down and privately discuss the issues you expressed very *publicly*, and some might say inappropriately, in that meeting?"

Set guidelines for communication. It's difficult when you are being yelled at to find your footing. To regain control of the situation, Gary and Ruth Namie, authors of *The Bully at Work*, suggest saying something along the lines of, "Let's talk about this. You go first and I won't interrupt. Then when you're done, I'll see if I have any questions."[8]

Don't take it lying down. If your boss gets angry and volatile, while you don't want to pick a fight or further instigate them, you also shouldn't let him/her get away with such abusive behavior. Try diffusing the situation by saying, "I can't speak to someone

---

8. Namie and Namie, *The Bully at Work*, p. 32.

who yells at me, and when you can speak to me at a normal deci-
bel, I will be happy to come back to your office and talk to you."
This might seem like a gutsy move, but it will empower you and
show your boss that you aren't a doormat.

Ask questions. Susan Futterman, author of *When You Work for a
Bully,* and the founder of MyToxicBoss.com, suggests saying
something like, "In what way does calling me a moron or idiot
solve the problem?"[9]

The Blamer

When a problem arises, the Blamer is more concerned about
placing the blame elsewhere than finding a solution. This kind
of boss loves to point fingers, and will spend tedious amounts of
time trying to figure exactly who messed up. In short, the
Blamer blames in an effort to absolve him/herself of any responsibility.

Beating the Blame Game. The good news is that there are
ways to beat the Blame Game and keep yourself from having to
play defense. Here's how:

Keep everything in writing. Keeping everything documented
protects you. With complete documentation, you can be sure that
you won't be held responsible for a mistake you didn't make. It's
the cardinal office rule of having a paper trail.

Camille, 24, a researcher at a financial services firm in New
York, had a boss who was always pointing fingers, and she found
documentation to be a good tactic. "He would constantly accuse

---

9. Gerri Willis, "Dealing with an Abusive Boss," CNNMoney.com, October 15,
2004. money.cnn.com/2004/10/15/pf/saving/willis_tips/index.htm

me of not doing things or following through on projects he never even mentioned to me. Having a paper trail was enormously helpful in defusing his constant blaming."

Don't apologize unnecessarily. As tempting as it might be to apologize in such a situation, try not to fall into this trap, lest you become, as one young woman pointed out, a "sorry machine." Many New Girls commented that this approach undermined them because they were taking blame for things that weren't their responsibility, becoming an easy target. If you work for a Blamer, rather than apologizing, make it clear that you were never given direction on that aspect of the project. Remember, if you apologize for everything, your boss will begin to believe it's your fault. Only apologize for things that are really your responsibility.

Find strength in numbers. If you're having problems with your blaming boss, chances are that other co-workers are as well. If possible, band together to protect one another.

After months of accepting blame from her boss, Arya teamed up with another young woman at her office who was having a similar problem. "Take a lesson from us," she says. "Don't go at this kind of boss alone, if at all possible." Arya and her co-worker agreed beforehand, that if their boss blamed one of them for something, both of them would accept responsibility.

The Silent Saboteur
At first you think, "What a nice woman! I'm sure she is going to help me out." This is the kind of boss, however, who will work with you on a project, all the while giving you the impression that

everything is going fine. Then, during your evaluation, you'll learn from *his/her* boss that he has been disappointed in your performance.

Abigail worked for a Silent Saboteur who was responsible for getting her fired. "I slaved day and night on this project for her, and the whole time she never said a word to me about my performance on the project, leading me to believe that I had done a good job. Imagine how surprised I was when out of nowhere my boss called me into his office on Monday morning and said he going to have to terminate me because 'Marcy' [her direct report] had no confidence in my work. I couldn't believe it. How could this woman, who never said a word to me about my performance, and always acted so nice to my face, have done this?"

Surmounting the Silent Saboteur. Since this type of boss is slightly more under-the-radar, it's important to have some good strategies. Some tried-and-true ones that worked for the many young women who've worked for the Silent Saboteur:

Always ask for written feedback. If you suspect you're working with a sabotaging boss, don't stop at documenting your work. After each project, ask for written feedback, whether it's formally or informally. This way, if a boss goes behind your back, you'll have a paper trail if he/she changes his/her story.

Don't be misled by niceness. At first, this type of boss may win you over by expressing kindness and concern—as if he/she is looking out for you. It's easy to misinterpret niceness for genuine concern. It's only after the person has gained your trust that you'll start noticing the repercussions of his/her sabotaging ways. The first few times this happens, you may be tempted to justify unacceptable behavior by saying, "But, oh, she's so nice" or "But he really seems like he wants to help me." But by letting this type of behavior continue, you could be sabotaging your own chances of success.

Be assertive. If your boss is silently sabotaging you, articulate his/her behavior.

When you point out this behavior, it doesn't have to be overly aggressively, especially if you simply make a direct statement, such as, "You aren't answering my question."

If a boss is acting passive-aggressive, say to him/her, "For us to have an effective professional relationship, I need you to be clear with me so we can work together to meet the goals of this project."

The Jekyll-and-Hyde

Working with this boss can leave you feeling hot and cold. One minute this boss is taking an interest in you personally and soliciting your opinion about big, important projects but then, in a heartbeat, becomes cold or abusive, throws large amounts of work at you, and berates you for your performance. Jaya, 30, the former director of a nonprofit in New York, found that her Jekyll-and-Hyde boss would send glowing e-mails praising her abilities and hours later blow up at her.

Getting beyond Jekyll and Hyde. Dealing with the Jekyll-and-Hyde boss is all about finding the delicate balance between putting your foot down when he/she is out of line, but also harnessing the positive aspects of your relationships.

Confront your boss about erratic behavior. Explain to your boss that the hot and cold way he/she manages you adds a layer of volatility to the workplace that is creating an additional hurdle at work. Ask if you could work together to figure out a better way to accomplish your tasks. Also, use your personal relationship as leverage here. Say something along the lines of, "Sue, we have a great personal relationship, but I'm wondering what are some things we both could do to improve our professional relationship." Also, offer your own suggestions and solutions. For example, say something like, "I know I could do the following things to improve the professional side of our relationship . . ." That might make your boss more amenable to offering his/her own suggestions.

Let your boss know you appreciate positive feedback. By responding actively to positive feedback, you'll encourage your employer to keep giving it. Camille says it's an approach that worked for her. "When I worked for a hot-and-cold boss, I made a point, in a non-kiss-ass way, to tell her that I appreciated it when she encouraged me. It definitely minimized some of her hot/cold behavior."

The Boss Friend

With all this talk about bad bosses, there will also be bosses that you become friends with, which poses an entirely different set of issues. The Boss Friend takes you under his/her wing and is like a brother or sister figure, but it's also clear who wields more power in the relationship. And while having a friendship with a superior can be great (there's nothing like socially lubricating a business relationship), it's still a workplace relationship that you've got to be savvy about.

Fielding the friendship. The key thing to be aware of here is that he/she is still your boss. Therefore:

Always maintain a level of professionalism. This means not divulging everything about your personal life; limiting the amount you gossip together; and not confiding your deepest, darkest secrets. First and foremost, this person is your boss and it's important that he/she views you as a professional, not as the girl who can't stop talking about her problems. Beware, because it's easy to get carried away in a boss friendship. It's difficult to say where the boundary is between friend and boss, particularly when it involves personal matters, but a good barometer is: "Would I want my boss's boss to know this about me?"

Don't let things slide because your boss is your "friend." Susan says she had a difficult time setting boundaries with her Boss Friend. "I would use the excuse that we were friends so she would understand if I had to leave early or couldn't meet a deadline. This ultimately proved to be a bad approach because it undermined my professional relationship with her."

Just because your boss is your friend, it's not license to take advantage and start slacking, because that will ultimately erode both your professional and personal relationship.

Don't act like your boss is your best friend. Many young women talked about feeling very flattered when an older, more senior person took an interest in them. However, as they all cautioned, you don't want to step out of bounds, so take the cues from your superior. In practical terms, this probably means you don't want to wait outside this person's office everyday eagerly waiting for him/her to invite you to lunch. That doesn't mean that you should never ask your boss to have lunch, drop by his/her office, or go out for coffee; just modulate these activities. Don't presume that your friendship is automatically your Boss Friend's priority; he/she has a job to do, and that may mean not socializing with you within the office environment.

The Predator

The Predator is typically an older, male boss who is somewhat duplicitous. On one hand, he shows a genuine interest in trying to help you in your career; but on the other, he seems ready and willing to take advantage of you. Take, for example, Beth, 24, now a researcher at a national relief agency, who was frantically searching for a job after college. She stumbled across "Barry." Barry was what everyone hopes to find when they are trying to get hired—he was extremely well connected, and generously offered to tap all of his resources to help Beth get a job. During the process, he took her out to lavish dinners and invited her over to his house to schmooze. Ultimately, Barry found Beth a job at his company. He continued to take her out to dinner and invite her over to his house. Curiously, his wife was never home during those times. After Beth had been at the company for about six months, Barry invited her out for yet another lavish dinner. There he professed his romantic interest, telling her he couldn't go on in their platonic state. Beth, totally flabbergasted, didn't know what to do.

Preempting the Predator. Dealing with a Predator boss is all about being straightforward.

Set boundaries with him early on. If you sense your boss is interested in your romantically, make it clear to him from the outset that you aren't interested in pursuing anything beyond a professional relationship. While it may be difficult to draw a boundary with a boss who is making romantic or sexual advances toward you, it's much harder to backpedal out of a situation that's gotten out of hand.

Rory, a research assistant at a think tank in New York, had biweekly lunch meetings with a higher-up in another department. "We would have these casual, professional lunches, but one time he asked me to send him some pictures of myself. He told me he wanted to be able to look at me when I wasn't there."

In an e-mail requesting these pictures, he made it clear that he had the desire and connections to help Rory further her career in the field. Feeling confused and vulnerable, Rory sent him pictures of herself. "I was worried that if I didn't, he might not help me. I didn't want to alienate someone who had so much potential to help me in my career." Clearly, Rory didn't make the best choice in setting professional boundaries.

Instead, Rory could have set the boundaries immediately by stating, in a polite, firm way, "I know you don't mean any harm, but I don't think that it's appropriate for you to have a picture of me."

Don't get romantically involved. This all goes back to a workplace rule we've already covered: Don't get romantically involved with your boss. Remember Beth and her boss, Barry? Despite her initial shock at Barry's advances, the two started a romantic relationship. Beth ultimately regrets that decision. "It became problematic because he was my older boss and people

started to question my cushy assignments. It definitely was a
thorny work situation."

Bottom line: Don't give in to a Predator's advances, no matter
how flattering they appear. This is a dangerous pattern to start
early on in your career.

Don't rely on him for professional favors. Even though he
may offer, the less you rely on him for favors, the easier it will be
to pull away. Young women who have been in this situation warn
other New Girls to minimize what you ask of a Predator. If you
find yourself in this type of situation, try to create more of a
boundary by minimizing your obligations to him. If you let him
go out of his way for you and accept favor after favor, you are
putting yourself in an even more vulnerable and indebted position, not to mention risking losing the respect of your co-
workers.

Human Resources Debunked

While your Human Resources department might seem like some
vague entity that is just there to process your paperwork, they can
be very helpful to you, particularly when it comes to bad-boss situations. So if you're experiencing any of the problems covered in
this chapter and the situation has gotten out of hand, arrange a
meeting with your Human Resources department to discuss how
to solve it.

But Human Resources isn't only there to help you solve problems; it can also aid you in advancing your career. Gabrielle
Glore, who now runs her own marketing and event-planning com-

pany, got fast-tracked when she was just starting out by always keeping her HR department abreast of what she was doing.

Tips to make Human Resources work for you

Like almost everything at the office, you've got to take advantage of what your Human Resources offers, to get results. Here are some tips to make Human Resources work for you:

- Make it a point, upon starting your job, to introduce yourself to your Human Resources liaison.

- Check in with Human Resources every six months. Ask them about concrete things you can do to meet your career goals. For example, if you want to be promoted to assistant manager in six months, ask them what they would suggest are the best ways to go about achieving that goal.

- Inquire who the five or ten higher-ups are at the company to whom you should make a point of introducing yourself.

- If you are having a problem with a bad boss and you want to report it to Human Resources, bring documentation. Approach the situation by saying something like, "I want to work with my boss, but these things are standing in the way." Avoid coming off as overly negative and saying such things as, "I hate my boss. He's such a jerk."

Note to Current and Future Bosses:
Nice Is the New Mean

As previously noted, working for an unsupportive boss can take a serious mental and physical toll on your work life. A 2005 British study on retaining female employees found that having a supportive boss was the single most important factor in retaining female staff.[10] The article stated that women chose a company and decided to stay or leave depending on three key factors: having supportive managers (63 percent), having some kind of assistance with family and personal obligations (54 percent), and flexible working hours (50 percent). On the hit Bravo show *Project Runway*, when the few remaining contestants asked Fern Mallis, vice president at IMG Fashion, the company that produces Olympus Fashion Week, if there was anything the contestants could have done differently, Mallis said, "You can never go wrong being nice. Being the drama queen and having a fit doesn't make anyone want to do anything for you. You can never go wrong being nice and helpful."

Katherine, 24, who worked for cosmetics entrepreneur Bobbi Brown, experienced this firsthand. "Even when something goes awry, Bobbi keeps her cool and doesn't get upset. Recently, she was looking at a photo that we were going to use for her book *Living Beauty*, and she didn't like the earrings on one of the models. If that was my old boss, we would have all been nailed to the wall. Instead, Bobbi was great about it." Although sometimes it's hard to figure out if your potential new boss is going to be a tyrant, do your research to avoid such negative situations. Ask previous employees, current employees, and anyone else with valuable insight. This might mean you have to read between the lines when

10. Lucy Sheriff, "Nice Bosses Retain More (Female) Staff," *The Register,* April 20 2005.

someone says to you, "Barry likes to spend a lot of 'personal' time with new female hires," but it's reading (and research) well worth doing.

Finally, there is a great new management technique presented by Linda Kaplan Thaler and Robin Koval in their compelling book *The Power of Nice*. It's a management technique that has made their ad agency, the Kaplan Thaler Group, one of the fastest growing in the country, with almost a billion dollars a year in billing. And while their approach makes good sense, it is hardly just touchy-feely. "Nice" actually generates more money, as they point out in their book: "According to Professor Daniel Goleman, a Harvard psychologist, there is a direct correlation between employee morale and the bottom line. One study found that every 2 percent increase in the service climate—that is, the general cheerfulness and helpfulness of the staff—saw a 1 percent increase in revenue."[11]

Not only is nice the new mean, but it also has a powerful impact on the bottom line, something bosses everywhere should get hip to.

11. Daniel Goleman, Richard Boyatzis, and Annie McKee, *Primal Leadership: Realizing the Power of Emotional Intelligence* (Boston: Harvard Business School Press, 2002), p. 15.

TAKEAWAYS

- Be assertive. Taking action against bad boss behavior early will save you trouble later on.

- Learn how to use Human Resources to your advantage. Human Resources can be helpful when you're having a problem, but they can also be just as helpful in advancing your career.

- Draw the line if a superior shows you inappropriate personal attention.

- Keep in mind the Power of Nice, and what a bottom line impact it has.

CHAPTER FIVE

Even Serena and Venus Williams Have a Coach
Where, Why, and How to Find a Mentor

Now that you know how to deal with all the people at the office who can potentially make your life difficult, let's talk about the people who are going to help you. And you will need help. As Jean Otte, the founder and CEO of Women Unlimited, a leadership development mentor program and the author of *Changing the Corporate Landscape: A Woman's Guide to Cultivating Leadership Excellence*, puts it, " No one does it alone. Even Tiger Woods has a coach. So start thinking—and looking—for a group of people that can give you support, insight, and guidance as you navigate the early years of your career. To clarify, these aren't your girl-friends; it's more about finding support to help you develop pro-fessionally and reach your career goals, than about creating camaraderie in the trenches.

These people are most commonly referred to as *mentors*. You've probably heard this nebulous term tossed around. You might have heard of it in the context of that formal mentoring program that your friend participates in at her big, fancy corporate job, or from that guy who rose through the ranks ridiculously fast and credits it all to his "mentor." By definition, a mentor is someone who will serve as a trusted counselor or teacher. But it's often more complicated than that. This chapter will provide information about why you need a mentor, how to go about finding one, and what to do and what not to do once you've found your team of mentors.

What people forget to talk about is how a relationship with a mentor actually works. Cultivating a relationship with a mentor takes more than just saying to someone, "Will you be my mentor?" In most cases, the mentor relationship evolves organically.

A March 2000 *New York Times* article on the subject of mentoring, quoted the legendary 1979 *Harvard Business Review* study that found "nothing beats the human touch for learning how to navigate the shoals of workplace politics."[1] However, finding a mentor is often more difficult that it seems—especially for women. Jennifer Allyn, director of research and advisory services for Catalyst, a nonprofit research organization in New York that works to advance women in business, weighed in on the 2000 *Times* piece, saying, "Unfortunately, because the people at the top are still usually white men, they tend to mentor other white men."[2] Another difficulty is that women don't bond or socialize the way men can or do. Think about it. When was the last time you picked up golf clubs or a cigar? It's for these reasons, among others, that Otte says she doesn't see the mentor relationship coming as naturally to women. That's why you need practical tools, guidance, and insight to give you that edge.

1. Dylan Loeb McClan, "Management: As They Say, a Good Mentor Is Hard to Find," *New York Times*, March 8, 2000.
2. Ibid.

Why You Need a Mentor

Recent statistics and studies indicate why it's well worth your time both professionally, and economically, to put finding a mentor at the top of your list when you start any new job. In 2002, a survey by the Simmons School of Management found that women with informal mentors reported a greater number of promotions and a higher promotion rate than did those without mentors.[3] In 2003, Orlando-based Spherion recruiting group, in conjunction with Saratoga Institute, interviewed more than twenty thousand employees and found that a third said they'd leave their job within the first year if there were no provisions for mentorship.[4]

Women across the board reap the benefits of mentoring. JC Penney Company is a perfect example of how a good mentoring program can help women reach management positions much faster than they would without guidance. The February 17, 1997 cover story of *Business Week* was: "Breaking Through: How do some companies get ahead while so many miss the boat?" The article described, among others, the mentoring program at JC Penney. The mentoring program at JC Penney tapped women described as "upper-management candidates" who regularly had lunches and roundtable discussions with senior managers. The results were striking: At JC Penney, women now represent 26.6 percent of middle and senior managers, up from 18.9 percent in 1990.[5] An almost 8 percent increase in seven years! Similarly, Procter and Gamble, through its revamped mentoring program,

3. CGO Insights, Briefing Note Number 15, January 2003. www.simmons.edu/som/docs/centers/insights15.pdf
4. www.spherion.com/press/releases/2003/EWFrelease.jsp
5. Linda Himelstein, "Breaking Through: How do some companies help women get ahead while so many miss the boat," *Business Week*, February 17, 1997.

has improved its retention of talented women, and according to a 1998 article in *Fast Company,* the advertising division at Procter and Gamble was losing twice as many women as men. Since the launch of several mentoring initiatives in 1994, the rates have evened out."[6]

In addition to what the statistics and studies have found, mentors are crucial because they will help guide you through those rocky patches in your career. Becky Newman, the Associate Vice Chancellor of Development at the University of California, San Diego, is a mentor to many young women (and men) who come through her development office. Newman's take is this: "You have to figure out what the person you are mentoring needs. For instance, I had a young development officer and she was good at the numbers, but she needed work on developing personal relationships. So I took her along to meetings with long-term donors. We had a continual, ongoing review of where she was in her career." Newman is clearly the gold standard for a mentor. She realized the strengths and weaknesses of her mentee, and focused her energy on improving her weaknesses while promoting her strengths.

Mentors can also help make your career goals come to fruition. Bobbi Brown tells the incredible story of Sharice, a young woman she met selling soap at a local art fair. Brown fell in love with the soaps and hired Sharice to mass-produce them for Bobbi Brown Cosmetics. "Now we constantly run out of them. I set her up with the art and marketing department to help her package them." While this might seem like a fairy godmother story, Sharice took the initiative to follow up with Brown and set their partnership in motion, following carefully the steps

6. Alison Seiffer, "Women's Ways of Mentoring," *Fast Company,* Issue 17, September 1998. pf.fastcompany.com/magazine/17/womentoring.html

Brown instructed her to take. Sharice subsequently took the time to develop a product that would fit the needs of Brown's company. There's a good lesson to be learned here: Even if mentors *do* magically appear out of thin air at art fairs and solicit your work, you still have to follow up with them in order to make it happen.

Tricks of the Trade

Now you know why you need a mentor—but how can you go about getting one? It helps to have some great techniques for the (sometimes awkward) process of approaching a mentor. Dozens of the young women interviewed for *New Girl on the Job* said they were baffled by the mechanics of the mentor relationship, or found themselves dissatisfied with their company or organization's formal mentoring programs.

First, break out of the old model of mentor as an aged, wise sage that is going to take you under his/her wing as a protégé and escort you on a magic carpet ride to the CEO suite. When Jean Otte, founder of Women Unlimited, works with women at large corporations, she tells them to do away with "the listen-and-learn-and-you-can-be-like-me-one-day model." "The new model is that mentors come in many shapes, sizes, and ages."

Marianne, 25, started out working at a large bank in New York and was—like many young women—turned off by the formal mentoring program. "I didn't want to have to go to a woman's group. I wanted to have it casual, on a day-to-day basis. It shouldn't be something that you have to have in a separate group." Marianne identifies what many young women express about formal mentoring programs—they can often seem contrived. While they work for some, for others they feel forced and fake. Like a romantic relationship, Otte says, mentoring cannot be forced. "You can't just say to someone, 'go off and be a pair.' You have to have a mutual interest. The mentor has to feel that he, or she, has something to offer that person."

Like other young women, Christy, 26, an assistant at an entertainment company in Los Angeles, has found her company's formal mentoring programs to be extremely beneficial. "I've had a great experience with my mentor. I liked that it was a built-in system." The trick is to find a way to make a formal mentoring program work for you. Maybe it's singling out some specific person that you think you will vibe with, or tailoring the program to your needs and career goals.

Whatever you do, don't be tepid about pursuing a mentor relationship. Developing a relationship with a mentor often takes a lot of persistence on the part of the mentee. Christy learned quickly that you cannot be shy about e-mailing and calling. "You don't want to cross the line into being annoying. But your mentor is probably really busy and you are going to fall off the radar. With my mentor, I would send him two or three e-mails and not hear back. When I would run into him, he told me to just keep it up."

In a similar situation to Christy's, Myia, 27, a rising entertainment executive in New York, found that persistence worked to her advantage. She made it her mission to get in touch with a prominent woman in the entertainment field. "I called her a bunch of times, I wrote her e-mails, and I asked if I could do anything to volunteer in any of the organizations she was a part of. I finally ran into her at a seminar. She said to me, 'Oh, you are my stalker.' But then she invited me to a dinner she was hosting." Myia also used the tactic of finding a common ground with her mentors. "I had one mentor who I bonded with over *America's Next Top Model*, and when the show came back on the air, I sent her an e-mail about it and suggested that we have lunch." Myia's strategy is a great one. Maybe it's jazz, art, or reality TV—whatever the topic, it always strengthens the connection when you can find a common ground. So instead of just e-mailing your mentor and saying "hi," contact him/her with a specific topic. Try something like: "I just read this article in *USA Today* and it made me think of the conversation we had last week [and reference that conversation]" and then suggest you connect.

Dena, an attorney in Washington, D.C., says she has been brazen and proactive about building relationships with mentors. "I took a management class in office politics, and I was really impressed with the professor. So I chatted with her, got her e-mail address, and invited her to lunch, which I paid for. I talked to her about my goals and what I wanted to do. We now meet every couple of months."

Caroline Baum, an award-winning columnist for Bloomberg News and author of *Just What I Said*, agrees that it is great to say to someone, " 'Can I buy you a drink? I admire what you do.' If someone said that to me, I'd be flattered."

Kimberly, 28, who used to work for a large media conglomerate and now runs her own business in Los Angeles, says in retrospect she was too afraid to ask for people's time. "I thought that I was so low on the totem pole that no one cared about me, but I've learned that anyone who is invested in their company should care about the young workforce moving up. I found that when I finally reached out to people, they were responsive and responded very positively."

Another good thing to keep in mind as you cultivate relationships with mentors is that mentoring should be about soliciting advice and feedback, not about stroking your ego.

In 2005, *Forbes* magazine ran a piece on the basics of mentoring and they made the following critical point: "Mentoring should be a two-way street. It's not all about you, your problems and your career. Think about why you need a mentor and how the mentor would benefit from spending time with you. Then approach the person, but don't come across as needy."[7] Some critical don'ts include:

- **Don't expect your mentor to be available whenever a crisis springs up or you have a dilemma.** Instead, be selective about the situations when you call on your mentor for crisis intervention. That way, he/she will really come through for you when you need it, and it won't seem like you are always on the precipice of a crisis.

- **Don't whine or complain about office politics and minutia on a regular basis.** Instead, temper the negative with the positive. Your mentor isn't a receptacle for all your complaints about the office.

- **Don't put all the responsibility on your mentor to initiate meetings, lunches, or reviews.** Instead, be proactive about setting up meetings and scheduling reviews. Show that you value your mentor's

7. Julie Watson, "Help Wanted: Mentors," *Forbes*, December 15, 2005.

time and are equally invested in the relationship.

- **Don't be shy.** Instead, be forward about setting up meetings, and come prepared with specific questions and points to talk about. You want to show your mentor that you value his/her time and you aren't just there to shoot the breeze.

"Will You Be My Mentor?" Is a Bad Pickup Line—How to Say It Better

What's the best way to approach someone about being your mentor? It's an issue worth giving some thought to, as you are probably not the only person seeking a potential mentor's guidance and time. Here are some choice picks from some mentoring pros:

- When it comes to approaching a mentor, Soledad O'Brien, anchor of CNN's *American Morning*, suggests taking the specific route, such as:

"Can we meet for twenty minutes on Friday so you can give me some pointers on how to write better leads for political pieces?"

- Kathleen Borges, whose company runs formal mentoring programs for companies such as Hewlett Packard, advises people to use the term "mentor" carefully:

"The term 'mentor' might confuse some people. They might not know what you're asking them to do." Other people might not view themselves as mentor material. Borges suggests that using the term "coach" might lighten the mood and connotation.[8]

• Jean Otte of Women Unlimited says that she is often put off when people call her and ask, "Will you be my mentor?"

"I'll be more responsive to someone if they ask me, 'Could I come and spend a little time with you and get your ideas and thoughts?' " That is a much different approach and is a lot less threatening to the person being asked. Remember, the most complimentary thing is to be asked for advice. So think about saying something like, "I'm not familiar with the financial aspects of the business. Would you mind sitting down with me to help me get a better handle on it?' "

• Kimberly suggests planning ahead and coming up with specific questions and issues:

"I prepared a lot for my meetings with my mentor. I spent a lot of time brainstorming questions and topics. I didn't want to waste their time. If I had an idea, or a project that I wanted to be a part of, I would write a mini-proposal to run by them. It's been very well received."

8. Therese Droste "Mentor, Anyone? Tips on the tricky proposition of identifying and working with mentors." *Women Connect*, February 29, 2000. www.women-unlimited.com/

- Like Kimberly, Christy also has a list of questions
  prepared for when she meets with her mentor:

"It's sort of like a first date so you want to come prepared
with stuff to talk about."

It Shouldn't Always Be Warm and Fuzzy

When seeking out a mentor, you don't want someone who only
tells you that you are great and wonderful; you need someone who
is willing to give you constructive feedback. Sonya Lockett, vice
president of Public Affairs at BET, says that, coming into the
workforce, many envision a mentor as someone who takes them
under his/her wing in a nurturing parent-daughter relationship.
"In my experience, it hasn't always been that 'cuddly.' Before I
came to BET, I worked at nonprofit. I was upset about the direction of the organization, and I was voicing my displeasure and
making a real stink. There was a female board member who kind
of looked out for me. She pulled me aside and told me that I really
should reconsider the way I was acting. She was very specific and
said, 'If you go talk to this person, this person, and that person,
and say what the problem is, you are going to get the results you
want. Right now you aren't coming across well.' I argued with her
for a minute, but then I took her advice."

Similarly, senior *News Hour* correspondent Judy Woodruff
advises young women to find someone who will give honest
answers when asked, "How am I doing?" or "How does my work
look?" "Early on in my career, I tried to do that. I asked people
all the time, 'How am I doing?' I had one guy tell me that I needed

to work on my voice. He was the only person who told me that. Later on, when I applied for a job at NBC, he said that I needed to work on my Southern accent. He said, 'You sound like you are reporting on a tea party.' That's the kind of advice everyone needs."

Marjory Kaplan runs the Jewish Community Foundation, the largest foundation in San Diego. When she mentors young women, her strategy is to give them open and honest criticism. "I think you have to find a mentor who really cares about you and isn't afraid to give you feedback. I told this one young woman who spoke in a very 'girly' high-pitched voice, that I wanted her voice to mimic the great work she was doing." Although it's never pleasant to hear criticism, the repercussions of not hearing it are often far worse. Plus, a mentor can show you how to improve your weak areas. It's like having personal trainers. You don't have to see them every day but, when you do see them, you want them to address your weak spots.

What Should I Look For in a Mentor?

Not just anyone should be your mentor. You have to look for someone who is going to help you achieve your professional goals. First, you want to seek out someone who is open to you and *wants* to be a mentor. Interior designer Ellie Cullman, co-founder of interior design firm Cullman & Kravis, is a model of this. Her mentoring strategy is, "Be nice to people, don't be dictatorial, and be understanding." Cullman also recognizes the cardinal management principle: you get back what you put into people. "It's amazing for me to see people develop and for them to go on to juggle so many responsibilities." That's another crucial thing—if you have a boss, or mentor, who starts to get resentful as you take on more responsibility, you probably don't want that person to be a guiding force in your career. You want a mentor who wants you to have wings.

Gwenn Speak, vice president of Planit M modeling agency, is another example of a gold-standard mentor. Speak is known for taking young women off the reception desk and mentoring them to become agents. She advocates using the "Mini-me" method: "My advice to young women when it comes to looking for a mentor is to find someone who is the best at what they do, and eat what they eat for breakfast. I was clever enough to copy the right person. Now, I have someone who does everything I do. She is like a 'Mini-me' now. I modeled myself on my boss. It sounds like an annoying strategy, but it's not. The younger women at the office think, 'Oh, Gwenn gets here early, so should I.' "

In the vein of becoming a "Mini-me," question your mentors about their interests, involvement in the community, and activities outside of work. This is what Myia does. "I always ask my mentors about what organizations and clubs they belong to. I've learned about a lot of great organizations by asking my mentors this question. Plus, if this is a person that you really want to be like, it helps to figure where they spend their time."

You also want to look for someone who is going to challenge you. Essie Chambers, executive director of development at Noggin, attributes her steady (and fast) climb up the ladder to her mentor. "I think it's because of her that I got promoted every year. She has been great about giving me opportunities that are a reach for me."

Jill Herzig, executive editor of *Glamour* magazine, advises finding someone on your team who gets you and who knows you inside the workplace. "The best mentor to pick is someone who is dealing with you a lot. The person who sees you strut your stuff."

On a more touchy-feely note, you want to connect with a mentor who believes in you. Lisa Witter, general manager of Fenton Communications, was given the responsibility of running the New York office when she was 27 because her boss believed in her. "My mentor, David Fenton, took a chance on me. He just let me go for it. He trusted my judgment."

Fiona, 30, an architect in New York, has found that it's critical to find someone who explains the "why" to you. "When my mentor shows me a drawing of a house, she'll explain to me all the reasons *why* it is amazing."

A Good Mentor Should . . .

- Encourage your success

- Foster your ideas

- Help you shine

- Explain the "whys" to you

- Challenge you with new projects and opportunities

- Be someone whose job you would one day want to have

- Believe in your abilities

Have More Than One Mentor

Why limit yourself to one mentor? You can't put all your stock in just one person. You probably need five, eight or even ten mentors. People who rise to the top have a team—a board of directors, a group of advisors—whatever you want to call it. Very successful people probably have one person they go to for financial advice, another they go to for more creative guidance, and another they go to for navigating office politics. It's unrealistic to expect one person to guide every aspect of your work life.

From the first day you enter a job, you want to think about how you can create a network of people that will support you. Soledad O'Brien, CNN correspondent, says it's a strategy that helped her get where she is today. "I was really happy to have mentors who were working mothers, but I also had mentors who were guys, who didn't want to talk about working mothers." As reported by a January 2004 *New York Times* article, a study of members of racial minorities at three large corporations by David A. Thomas, a Harvard Business School professor, found that the most successful had a strong network of mentors.[9]

As you build your team of mentors, think about diversifying. For example, have one mentor from work, one male, one female, one college or graduate school professor, one person of your same generation, one person who is a generation removed. Essentially, you want to surround yourself with a broad-based team of people who support you.

9. Perry Garfinkel, "Executive Life; Putting a Formal Stamp on Mentoring." *New York Times*, January 18, 2004.

Some Final Nuts and Bolts

Don't pigeonhole who can and can't be your mentor. Jean Otte, in her national mentoring programs for Women Unlimited, says she never matches women who are from the same background. "I don't put finance with finance people. I put IT people with sales people. You can't think of yourself in one isolated capacity. Too often women get stuck in the mentality, 'I'm in sales, I'm in marketing, I'm in HR.' What they really have in common is that they are all business people. I think that is one of the reasons that I am successful. I went in with the understanding that I'll learn from everyone."

It all goes back to the main point that no one does it alone. We can benefit from guidance at all stages of our career, but particularly at the beginning when the learning curve can be steep.

TAKEAWAYS

- When you meet with your mentor, come prepared with a list of questions, goals, objectives, and so on. It's like a first date—you want to have stuff to talk about.

- Don't make it all about what your mentor can do for you. Draw your mentor out. Ask about his/her experience in the field, how he/she got interested in the industry, and how his/her take on the the industry has changed. Like any relationship, it's about give and take.

- Be persistent but don't be a nudge—mentors are busy people.

- When seeking out mentors, reach out to a wide variety of people. Don't get stuck in a smokestack. Just because you work in the finance department shouldn't prevent you from reaching out to someone in the tech department.

- Be specific. When looking for guidance, reach beyond vague phrases like, "Will you be my mentor?" Approach mentors with pointed questions, such as, "I really admire the way you handled that client call on Tuesday; can you meet with me this week to give me some pointers on that?"

- Mentoring isn't a singular concept. Build a team of people. You want to think about diversifying your team as much as possible. Reach across industry, race, and gender, to build the broadest team possible. Think about having a "go-to" person for each area: office politics, compensation, soft skills, and hard skills.

- Think outside the box. Don't assume that a mentor is going to be an old, wise, male sage—nor that a mentor for a young woman need be an older woman. The twenty-first-century workplace is about finding mentors in all shapes and sizes.

CHAPTER SIX

Mistakes Happen
Dealing with Failures and Feedback

There are four words that every New Girl dreads: "You made a mistake." When (not if) this happens to you, you will invariably have some version of this reaction: "How could I have messed this up? It should have been a no-brainer!"

Welcome to the office! It's that strange subuniverse where suddenly you become incapable of getting even some of the most simple tasks right, which makes you doubt yourself and your abilities to do the job. Although making a mistake is never pleasant, it's really not as bad as it seems. Office life requires a different set of skills that, as a New Girl, you are in the process of cultivating. It might be difficult, but the best way to recover from a mistake is to treat it as part of your ongoing New Girl education.

Constructive criticism can help us learn more about ourselves. It should not define us; criticism is just one person's perception of us. Katie Couric, the first female anchor of a network evening news program, was told during the early years of her career that she would never make it on air. Makeup maven Bobbi Brown had similar experiences and doubts about herself at the beginning of her career, but she persevered. "I remember one guy telling me that I didn't have what it took to go into high-fashion makeup. Years later, he ended up hiring me."

Ideally, you should try to take criticism with a grain of salt. There will, however, be tough times, and it's helpful to have some survival tactics on hand to get through them.

Messing Up, Down, Around, and All Over the Place

Molly, 24, a medical student in New York, is well acquainted with making mistakes. "I get yelled at constantly at the hospital and I tend to take things very personally. I get yelled at by doctors, nurses—by everyone. You just have to have a thick skin." In developing her thick skin, she took a cue from an interaction she'd seen between two of her male colleagues: A male co-worker of hers made a mistake that was easily correctable, but was lambasted for it by a supervising doctor. A few minutes later, however, the two had forgotten the incident entirely and moved on. Molly observed, "If a woman had been yelled at like that, she probably would have taken it more personally, then maybe have held a grudge, and not been as able to be in such a neutral place." Molly learned not to let her mistakes appear to affect her confidence and capabilities, and to move on as quickly as she could.

Leslie, 22, when she was a reporter for a local newspaper in New York, made a mistake when she put off calling a source for a big story. As a result, she couldn't get the quote she needed. "I got reamed out for that. You have to learn, though, to sit up straight and say 'I'm sorry.' " Leslie also makes the good point that, just because you screw up or get yelled at, it doesn't mean that you are a bad worker. "It just means that in that one situation you dropped the ball."

Olivia, a financial analyst in New York, learned quickly that you can't *outsource the blame*. "I think it's important for the people you work with to realize that you will take responsibility for things. It's a quality my co-workers and superiors really value."

The reassuring thing is that everyone who is new (and old) on a job screws up once in a while. Jennifer Baumgardner, author of *Manifesta: Young Women, Feminism, and the Future*, at her first job at *Ms.* magazine, accidentally threw away necessary paperwork relating to the apartment her boss had just bought. Her advice to New Girls is, "If you make mistakes, you have to learn from it. They are horrifying, though. I apologized profusely when I threw out that important document. However, I wasn't afraid to take responsibility." That seems to be the bottom line from everyone who has botched things up at the office: own up to the mistake.

Jill Herzig of *Glamour* advises you to convey to your boss that you take it seriously when you make a mistake. "My assistant made a mistake that resulted in me not arriving at a place on time and making dozens of people wait. When I first brought this up with her, not in an angry way, because I pretty much was sure she would know instantaneously how bad this was, she was a little Teflon about it and said 'I'm sorry' and offered some solution, which is a good thing. Then, later on, we talked about it again. She let me know how upset she was about it—she was crying." In a situation such as this, Herzig advises young women to find a middle ground between the two reactions. "Her first reaction was a deer in the headlights, and she froze. The second was tears, which I completely understood, and in a way appreciated because it was clear she understood. The perfect compromise is to say right off the bat, 'Wow, I'm really sorry. I realize this is a huge problem. Is there anything I can do to fix it? What can I do to help out?' "

There is a clear line between owning up to mistakes and dwelling on them. Modeling agency vice president Gwenn Speak advises young women to minimize the time they spend obsessing over their mistakes. "One of the best qualities with my boss—a woman—is that we can yell at each other but, when it's over, we've hashed it out and I don't really think about it. If you keep thinking about your failure, or your issues, or your rejections—and there is a lot of rejection in the workplace for twenty-somethings—you'll never get ahead. It's like the football field: I get tackled, but then that same person is helping me up." Remember, you can completely erase one negative encounter with one positive encounter.

While mistakes are an inevitable part of a job, there are ways to avert a total and complete disaster. Juliana Evans, a manager in the public relations department at a large news station, believes one of the biggest mistakes new hires make is that, when things start to go south, they don't speak up. "If I've told some-one that I need to talk to 'Ed' at three and you haven't gotten in touch with him to set up an appointment and it is that after-noon, you need to speak up soon and say that things aren't going well."

One innovative way to deal with slip-ups at the office is an approach pioneered by Ellie Cullman, cofounder of interior design firm Cullman & Kravis, who manages dozens of young women, uses a technique that she calls *the Megillah,* a Hebrew term that refers to the idea of a biblical scroll. "We have some-thing in the office called the Megillah, which is: when something bad happens, you have to e-mail the whole office and tell them. The thought was, we would all develop an institutional memory so that rather than each person just making a mistake, we could all learn from it." Particularly in an industry such as interior design, where there are so many details, and new hires are responsible for keeping track of many of these details, the Megillah provides a constructive outlet for airing, and learning from, mistakes.

Stop Thinking of Every Mistake as a Failure!

Although it can be tough to bounce back, you can't worry that every setback will define your career. Everyone will make mistakes or will not perform to the level she thinks she "should," but it's really all in how she deals with the aftermath that matters. Take Georgia, 27, who works in the research department at a nonprofit agency in Los Angeles. "I was in charge of this conference, and when we got the reviews back, I had gotten high marks from everyone except one person. I must have read that bad review over one hundred times. My colleagues actually made me rip it up."

Georgia is a perfect example of this epidemic. She took one negative comment and let it color the very successful conference she had put on. New Girls have to master the art of *changing the channel*—the acquired skill of moving on after something doesn't "go right," or else things will start to spiral downward.

When You Shouldn't Take No for an Answer

While changing the channel is an important skill to cultivate, it mustn't be confused with being passive.

Accepting no as a boundary was a common workplace issue voiced by many of the young women interviewed for this book. When author Jennifer Baumgardner was an intern at *Ms.* magazine and looking to move up the ranks, they told her it was company policy that no one from the intern group could be hired for a full-time position. For some, that might have been the end of the road. Baumgardner, however, thought her skills would be a valuable asset to the company and wrote a memo to the editor in chief about a position she wanted to create. "My memo detailed what I thought the job would entail, how long I thought it would last, how much money I would need, and the reasons why I thought I was qualified for the position. They hired me. It was one of the most powerful feelings I had in my life, creating my own job at *Ms.* at twenty-three."

Young women are groomed to believe that if they please their boss and do everything right, they will automatically reap the rewards of all their hard work. While this is true to some extent, in today's ultracompetitive workplace, you need a little more ammunition to get ahead.

As Dede Bartlett, former vice president of Corporate Affairs Programs at Altria Group, Inc., puts it, "You, as a young person in the workforce, assume that if you do things on time and efficiently good things will happen, but that is not the case." The reality is that you often have to fight really hard for what you want and, often, deserve. This was a lesson Caroline, an editorial assistant in New York, learned quickly. After working at her job for about a year, she had pursued many leads on new book projects and was labeled as a real up-and-comer in her group. "Given how proactive I had been during my first year, I thought I deserved to be promoted to assistant editor. However, when I had my review, my boss said that people don't get promoted to assistant editor after a year, but I knew it did happen. I even had examples I could point to. So I went to my boss and told him that even though he didn't think it was a big distinction, I thought it was. Finally, he talked to my other boss and they gave me the promotion, but I would never have gotten it if I had just accepted the way things were 'supposed' to be done." The lesson to be learned from Caroline's experience? It's fighting for things and not so easily taking no for an answer that actually gets you what you want.

Still not convinced?

Lauren, 26, a consultant, got involved with her company's campus recruiting program. At about the same time, she was starting to feel increasingly discouraged about her job and the lack of recognition she was receiving for her hard work. "I was carrying the workload of someone a few levels above my position, but I was getting the salary and respect of someone much lower. Because campus recruiting required really 'selling' people on the company, and I was feeling down about my job and the company, I deferred myself from the process. Then the head of global recruiting sent me a nasty e-mail for deferring from the process. I decided to set up a meeting with him, which, miraculously, he took. I wanted to explain to him, in person, why I had deferred. In that meeting, I told him that I didn't think I could effectively convince potential employees about all the company had to offer when I felt as undervalued as I did. Understanding where I was coming from, he made some calls for me and I got promoted."

It's this strategy of *going to bat for yourself*—asking for a raise, promotion, or lateral move when no one offers it to you—that has propelled someone like senior *News Hour* correspondent Judy Woodruff as far as she has gotten in her career. However, it wasn't always an easy road for her, either. "I was devastated a number of times, but my view was that you just keep going. You never take no for an answer, you pick yourself up and move on. A long time ago, someone said to me that the difference between people who are successful and the people who aren't is that the successful people have the same number of failures, they just keep going." Woodruff said she even had to plead with NBC to be their White House correspondent. "But I got the gig." And look where she is now!

Feedback: Don't Hide from It

Let's make something absolutely clear: there is a large distinction between asking for constructive feedback and letting your pleaser side take over. It is imperative to come across as someone who can handle problems and come up with good solutions. Soledad O'Brien, CNN correspondent, says that when she was new on the job, she handed in a script that her boss was less than pleased with. "I wrote this script and she reamed me out. So the next time I did something for her, I had a dialogue with her. I didn't hide from the criticism. People want to hear that you get it. We have a young woman who doesn't hide from the criticism and she just got promoted to producer because she always follows up

and asks for feedback. Ninety percent of what I like about working with her is that she takes full responsibility. But that sometimes means having an unpleasant conversation."

Kathy Bonk, co-founder of Communications Consortium
Media Center, notices that young women sometimes have difficulty taking criticism. "It flips them out that they aren't perfect."
You could certainly drive yourself crazy trying to be perfect all of
the time. Instead, try to get something out of the feedback. Bonk
urges, "Don't assume the feedback is being given in a punitive
way. People are just trying to make things better."

Too often young women are stereotyped as not being able to
take criticism. However, if you establish from the outset that you
are comfortable with the process of receiving feedback and even
solicit it from your colleagues, the stigma will dissipate. O'Brien
says that the people she works with really appreciate that she lis-
tens to feedback. "I always have people saying to me, 'Soledad, I
don't like it when you do this and this.'" So the next time someone gives you feedback, don't immediately assume it's because
they don't think highly of you. Oftentimes, people take the time to
give feedback so you can do better and because they care.

Neda, 23, when she was working at an online magazine in San
Francisco, learned just how critical it is to solicit feedback. "I
remember the first time I asked for feedback, I was sort of laugh-
ing and I said, 'I don't know if you like what I'm doing. What do
you need?' It took me too long to have that first conversation with
my boss but it was such a relief. My boss said I was doing great,
and then told me the stuff that he really liked and what he wanted
more of." As Neda's experience illustrates, feedback helped her
find the sweet spot between what you want to give an employer
and what they want from you. Carol Frohlinger, president of

Negotiating Women, Inc., an organization that provides training
and counseling to professional women, organizations, and associ-
ations, points out, "You don't want to let all the negative stuff
come out at your year-end review. No one likes to be hit with stuff
like that all at once. You want to get people to be specific about
how you are viewed on a regular basis."

Another valuable aspect of feedback is that it lets you know
the areas of your job in which you've been the most effective.
Frohlinger advises young women to make the feedback process as
informal as possible. "Soliciting feedback from your boss doesn't
have to be a big, formal process where you take them into a room
and sit them down. You can just say to your boss, 'What do you
think worked or didn't work in that meeting? What did you think
was effective about the way I did that presentation?' " As was the
case with Neda, you could be doing things that your boss values,
but have no idea about. Soliciting feedback on a regular basis lets
you know what you might be doing unconsciously and reinforces
you to repeat it consciously.

Presenting yourself as someone who is open and amenable to
criticism and feedback does have its limits. You don't want to let
yourself get *sandbagged*. Put simply, getting sandbagged is when
a supervisor or a boss hurls a litany of complaints at you with little warning. A situation like that is more likely to occur if you wait
until your year-end review to get feedback from your boss.
O'Brien says she was sandbagged early in her career when she
was working in San Francisco. "I got so upset after that meeting,
but it taught me a very important lesson. You cannot go into a
meeting without an agenda. Instead, in that situation, when he
started on his laundry list, I could have said, 'I'm really looking
forward to hearing about the feedback you have to offer me; let's

set up a time to have a meeting about that.' It's a good tactic to regain control of the meeting and give yourself the time to gather."

It Happens . . . Crying at Work

Unfortunately, making a mistake, getting caught off guard, or receiving negative feedback can spawn what every New Girl fears—crying. Usually, crying at the office is a result of some combination of emotional torment, lack of sleep, frustration, and too many hours spent staring at a screen trying to figure out how to format that PowerPoint presentation. There are many theories about crying at the office. A popular one, advanced by many, is the *hold it in at all costs* approach in which you keep your emotions in check while you are being reprimanded. This is the strategy Molly uses. "I'm so hyperaware of never crying at work. People get yelled at all the time, and girls cry all the time, especially in a field like surgery. You have to take it like a man."

Deborah Blum, a Pulitzer Prize–winning journalist, and author of *Sex on the Brain: The Biological Difference Between Men and Women*, makes a good point when she writes, "We'll have equality when it's accepted newsroom behavior to cry at your desk. Men don't sit around and cry at their desk. I'm not holding that as a model of behavior. I'm saying, who sets the standards for acceptable professional behavior?"[1] However, while you are in the midst of figuring out who sets the standards for acceptable office behavior, young women need to be prepared for how to handle this tic, which is exactly what crying at the office is—it's a tic,

1. Quoted in Ellen Barry, "Women's Work?" *Orlando Weekly*, November 19, 1998.

and the great thing about a tic is that it passes. Repeat: Crying is not a sign of mental instability.

While some people can hold it in, there may be those times when you can't. Catherine, 24, an associate at a private equity firm in New York, puts it into great perspective: "When the guys I work with get upset, they will punch or kick things. I explained to them that when I start to cry, that is just my reaction to feeling tired and frustrated. When I put it in that context for them, they suddenly got it."

Don't be fooled by the scientifically refuted premise that "women are just more emotional." According to the research of Vanderbilt University psychologist Ann Kring, whose findings on sex differences in emotion have appeared in the American Psychological Association's *Journal of Personality and Social Psychology*, "It is incorrect to make a blanket statement that women are more emotional than men. It is correct to say that women *show* more emotion than men."[2]

Glamour's Jill Herzig, like most people, doesn't think that showing emotion at work is great but doesn't view it as a dealbreaker on a job, by any stretch of the imagination. "So many people have cried to me that I can't even remember. I think too much is made of crying. It's really what you say while you are crying." It's also how you act after it happens. If you excuse yourself, compose yourself, and then come back and move on, it just won't be such a big deal.

To be fair, crying does have its roots in women's biological makeup. According to tear researcher William H. Frey II, a professor of pharmaceutics at the University of Minnesota, women cry four times as often as men—an average of 5.3 times per

2. "Men Just As Emotional As Women—If Only They'd Show It," Scinceagogo.com, June 20, 1998.

month, compared with 1.4 for men.[3] So while we are in the midst of creating an equal workplace and crying is still considered the biggest workplace taboo, here are a few tactics that might help you hold them back:

- Jut out your jaw. According to psychotherapist Larina Kase, "There is some evidence pushing your jaw forward interferes with the tearful response."[4]

- Chew gum to distract yourself.

- If you do let the flood gates open, don't deny it afterward by saying that it was "just allergies." Apologize for losing composure and move on.

- If you feel the tears coming, excuse yourself and say you need a moment to collect yourself.

- Try to focus on something else, such as the interesting book you just read, the funny movie you just saw, or what you are going to make for dinner.

Always Be Prepared

What no one tells you before you enter the workforce are those little tricks of the trade, or *cover yourself tactics* (CYT) that can help you avert many office disasters, and, most important, make you

3. Lorna Collier, "When a Good Cry Just Doesn't Work," *Chicago Tribune*, October 6, 2004.
4. Ibid.

look good to your boss and co-workers. It's the idea that small things make a big difference.

In many industries, the concept of *face time*—literally the amount of time people see you in the office, regardless of whether you are actually working or shopping on eBay—is the name of the game. So figure out from the outset (if possible) if your boss gets in early and leaves early, or gets in late and leaves late, so you are at your desk when he/she arrives. Particularly when you are the low woman on the totem pole, your boss wants to know that you are putting in equal, if not more, time than he/she is. Face time, while sometimes it just seems silly (why do you need to be there if you have nothing to do?) is just part of paying your dues.

Another great CYT is *offering solutions*. Christy, an assistant at a large entertainment company, learned to use this tactic early in her career. "When you approach your boss with a problem, have two or three solutions for it. [If your] boss is booked from ten to six and nothing in her schedule can be rescheduled, it's coming in and saying, 'Is nine an option? Can we move this?' Basically, it's just important to show that you have given it some thought."

Rachel, 28, an administrator at a private school in Los Angeles, got into a situation with a co-worker who was trying to blackmail her. She explains her tactic like this: "While the situation resolved itself, I kept track of every nasty e-mail he sent to me. That way, if the situation ever reared its ugly head, I would have proof about what transpired between us." In addition to always keeping a *paper trail*, Rachel learned the value of *progress reports*. "If you are working really hard, make sure everyone knows. I do this by sending progress reports. I'm in charge of the clubs at my school and I write these updates, and I make sure to cc the vice principal and principal on everything I do." It's these preemptive tactics, such as sending progress reports, that remind your boss that you are on the ball. Remember: no one is going to recognize you just because you are doing good work.

Figuring out how much or little your boss wants to know about your daily tasks is something you have to assess on a case-by-case base. The best approach is probably to sit down with your boss and figure out how you should keep him/her updated. You have to learn the style of each of your managers. For instance, you might have one boss who wants a whole detailed report, and another who just wants you to give him the five main points.

Neda has a good system. "Every Monday I e-mail my boss and lay out what I am planning on that week. I tell him what I am doing, and I ask him to tell me what he needs from me so we can figure out the work flow for the week. It's been really well received."

Although you don't want to ask your boss about every piece of minutia, making sure you are executing tasks correctly is very important. Dana, a construction manager, uses the *double-check method.* "When I'm not a hundred percent sure about something, I'll say, 'I think it is this,' but then I'll double-check. I run into this situation a lot in my line of work. My boss asked me how long it would take to get some material. I quoted him a time-frame that wasn't right, so I went back and double-checked and it turns out the time frame that I had quoted was way off. The minute I see that something I said isn't right, I'll say something. You always have to double-check."

Katherine, who spent her first couple years out of school working in the fashion industry, says that the most important thing she has learned that has helped her get where she is today (she now runs her own PR firm) is partially the *stay involved approach*. Staying involved means finding something valuable to do at the office—even if it's something as trivial as filing—rather than surfing the Net or reading a magazine.

"When I worked at Chanel, as an intern, I would constantly ask people if they had stuff for me to do, and if they didn't, they remembered me when they did. That is how you get opportunities—you need to be proactive." It's a strategy that paid off enormously for her. As an intern at Chanel, Katherine was asked to design an important mailing because her boss turned to her when she finally did need extra help.

Similarly, whether your title is assistant or senior vice president, you should always be thinking *beyond your job title*. This means thinking in terms of what value you can add to the job. It's not enough to just do the tasks that are assigned; you have to think if there are better ways to do them, what can be changed, omitted, and improved. Whether it's cutting out articles that relate to your new business strategy at your company, creating a more efficient and accessible database, or inquiring about a new area of research at your lab, it's the ultimate get-promoted-really-fast tactic: always be on your toes. The cliché goes "Dress for the job you want, not the job you have." Start thinking, "Work for the job you want, not the job you have." And even if you are answering phones and filing, you are privy to so much information—often valuable information that you can use to get ahead.

And finally, *always bring a pen.* Never go into a meeting without something to write with, lest you risk looking unprepared or—worse yet—uninterested. Mariana Sanchez, a brand manager at the powerhouse ad agency Saatchi and Saatchi, is always surprised at how often new hires go into meetings with nothing to write with. "It seems like such a minute point, but it's really an instant respect-getter or-loser."

Although making mistakes is an inevitable part of working, the confidence deflation that typically follows does not have to be. By owning up to our mistakes, soliciting feedback, going to bat for yourself, learning how to change the channel, and using some CYT, you'll ultimately be more prepared to handle any situation—from a work crisis to a work coup.

TAKEAWAYS

- Speak up early if you foresee things heading south. It's always better to give your boss the heads up about things taking a turn for the worse, than to have him/her be surprised. If you foresee a disaster, tell your boss so you can troubleshoot about ways to preempt it.

- If you see the same mistake happening again and again in your office, suggest implementing a system whereby you can all learn from each other's mistakes.

- Don't think of every little thing that goes wrong as a failure—treat it as a learning experience.

- When it comes to getting promotions or recognition, go to bat for yourself even if someone initially says no.

- Solicit feedback from your co-workers and bosses, and don't be afraid of a little negative feedback, as it's what might actually help you get ahead.

- Remember that crying is not a sign of mental instability and it happens to just about every woman at some point in her career. So if it happens to you, excuse yourself to the bathroom, compose yourself, and come back ready to move on.

- Remember: Always think beyond your job title.

CHAPTER SEVEN

Why Is She Being Such a Bitch?
How to Work with Women

The opening line of a 2002 Salon.com article about Phyllis Chesler's book, *Woman's Inhumanity to Woman,* leads in with the following anecdote. Chris Rock does a routine in which he instructs men on how to listen to a wife or girlfriend talk about her day. He tells men that paying attention isn't essential, just remember to look at her, nod your head, and at regular intervals say, "Uh-huh," "Really?" and "I told you that bitch was crazy."

Rock says that a woman, no matter what her profession, will always encounter another woman at work whom she's convinced is trying to ruin her life.[1] Obviously, this is exaggeration for the sake of entertainment, but if you talked to young women in today's workforce, you might begin to think that Rock's instructions are more than shtick. While Rock's routine certainly doesn't capture every woman's experience in the workplace, it rings true enough that it's well worth a chapter on how we can work better with our own kind.

The majority of young women interviewed for *New Girl on the*

1. Laura Miller, "Backstabbers," Salon.com, March 29, 2002.

Job echoed the observations of Arya, 24, a consultant: "You would think that women would stick up for each other, but they don't." It's why Jean Otte founded Women Unlimited. She refers to women's unwillingness to help other women as "the sad, sad situation with women in corporate America. Women aren't as conditioned to help each other. So many people in corporate America focus on the difficulties of working with male executives. My experience was that wasn't the major issue. I didn't have as many problems with my male executives as I did with my female executives."

An important disclaimer here—despite pervasive stereotypes, it's not just women who sabotage one another more in the workplace. Dr. Judith Briles, a Denver-based psychologist and recognized authority on women's issues, found that both women and men sabotage one another, but women are more inclined to be covert and more discriminatory in their style—e.g., talking about someone behind their back, spreading rumors, or "accidentally" excluding someone from an e-mail list. Conversely, men are more inclined to warn that an action is coming and are likely to take credit for the action.[2] In other words, women are more under the radar, whereas men let you know it is coming.

The images of backstabbing and competitiveness among women in the workplace are pervasive. Nan Mooney, the author of *I Can't Believe She Did That: Why Women Betray Each Other at Work*, found in her research that many young women come into the workplace unprepared to handle the relational aspect of working with other women. "There are going to be conflicts that arise, and there is going to be competition." How women handle these conflicts and confrontations is another issue. Until

2. Dr. Judith Briles, *Woman to Woman 2000: Becoming Sabotage Savvy in the New Millennium.* Far Hills, NJ: New Horizon, 1999.

recently, women's relationships in the workplace have been overlooked. But now, numerous books, articles, studies, and organizations are working to change that. This chapter will explore and offers solutions for what you, as a New Girl, could do to have better relationship with your female co-workers and supervisors.

Confrontation Is Not a Dirty Word

When Brittany, 23, a receptionist at an art gallery in New York, was training the new, young, female hire at the gallery, she found herself in an all too common New Girl situation. "I was training this girl and I felt like she wasn't appreciating anything I was saying. She wasn't thanking me. She was ignoring me and brushing me off. I was getting so offended. I started complaining about her to the other women."

Sound familiar? This is a situation so many women at work find themselves in. That is, tensions build with a female co-worker, and because women are generally socialized not to be as confrontational, situations spiral into a web of gossip, resentment, and passive-aggressiveness.

When Jennifer Baumgardner was working at *Ms.* magazine, tension began to mount with her slightly older female co-worker. "It seemed like all the senior editors liked her more. She kept hogging all the good comments at the meetings, and taking on leadership roles—it felt like she was stealing it from me. I told her that it felt like she was dominating. When we assessed the situation, she made the point that I wasn't asking for projects and leadership roles." Although it's easier to just write someone off as a "bitch," Baumgardner's situation illustrates that just because you feel animosity toward someone, doesn't mean it's not worth exploring.

Kara, 25, works closely with her female supervisor at a non-profit in Chicago. One day, when they were both facilitating a program, Kara's supervisor snapped at her—a result of mounting tensions that had been building up for months. It spawned what they both now jokingly refer to as their "first fight." Kara said, "A few days later we were eating lunch together and she said to me that she was really proud that I stood up for myself that day when I snapped back at her. That really got me over my fear of conflict."

The lesson to heed from all of this is that it is imperative to communicate with female co-workers, especially when you sense tension or conflict. Doesn't that sound like a better solution than gossiping behind someone's back, sabotaging her, or silently feeling threatened?

When It Gets Competitive, Bitchy, and Catty

When Jenny, 25, worked for a women's advocacy group in Washington, D.C., she had a *Why is she being such a bitch?* moment. "I had this one boss who was about ten years older than I was. I was doing really well and building relationships with a lot of the really senior people, and one day she called me into her office and told me that people don't like me because I'm too ambitious. The next week, when I was supposed to be out of the office, I came in and heard her and this other girl making fun of me. They were mimicking the way I spoke."

Rachel Simmons, author of *New York Times* best-seller *Odd Girl Out,* the first book to explore bullying between girls, advises that even if you hear horrible/nasty things about yourself, you don't want to burn bridges. "It's a small world and you should try to keep the relationship intact as much possible. Rather than yelling at or confronting your co-worker at the height of your anger, take some time to calm down and assess the situation. When you're ready to talk about it, say something along the lines of, "I felt hurt, violated, and embarrassed when I heard you talk about me." Simmons also points out that this is a good moment to differentiate between impact and hurt. "While someone might not have *meant* to hurt you, the impact they had is that they did." After you establish the impact that person's actions had on you, move on to talk about how you can effectively work together in the future. Frame the cattiness, gossip, or backstabbing in terms of how it is affecting your team and/or work product and what steps to take, so it doesn't impact on your job. Say something along the lines of, "This is not productive for you or me. Wouldn't it be more productive if we both spent less time focusing on our interpersonal issues and more time thinking about how to design better Web pages?"

While Jenny didn't necessarily burn her bridges, she didn't actively address the problem, either. "I should have said to them that I don't feel comfortable around them and let's figure out how to be each other's allies. Also, I shouldn't have personalized it as much I did. I took four days off of work."

The absence of a vocabulary to talk about these issues with female co-workers is often the root of the problem. The following are some tips for how to broach the issue of conflict with your female co-worker.

- Keep it focused on the work issue. Don't dwell on how
  she didn't invite you to lunch last week.

- Emphasize how much you both have to gain by being
  each other's allies. Particularly if you are a few of the
  lone females, you can say something like, "We really
  should be helping each other; look at how Tom and
  Dan band together."

- Even if you've gotten into a bad pattern of non-
  communication and gossiping about issues to your
  other co-workers, you can lead in with something like,
  "I know I haven't brought things up with you in the
  past, but I wanted to set a better standard for how we
  communicate. Here's what is on my mind."

With all this talk about getting along with our female co-
workers, it's important not to lose sight of the fact that it is okay
to be competitive. In fact, you need a healthy does of competitiveness to get ahead. It's just important to distinguish healthy
competition from playing dirty. You know: those things that just
make the office unpleasant for everyone. One way that Gwenn
Speak of Planit M modeling agency minimizes competition and
dirty play at her office is by separating responsibilities very
clearly. "I do this for two reasons. One, I want to know who is
accountable and, two, it has eliminated a lot of the competition."
Speak emphasizes that it's up to management to help monitor
the competition, to make sure it doesn't cross the line from
healthy to destructive. "You don't want to have ten people com-
peting for the same account. I think it is about management

knowing what is going on and not rewarding backstabbing behavior."

Not Everyone Is Going to Like You, and That's Really Just Fine

If your goal at work is to get everyone to like you, you might as well just quit now, because it's not a career-advancing strategy. The dozens of young women interviewed for *New Girl on the Job* all expressed some version of "I'm a people pleaser." At the office, however, being a people pleaser doesn't equal doing a good job. Sonya Lockett, vice president of Public Affairs for BET, has an empowering view. "My take is that you can be liked and respected at the same time. Also, everyone can like you and you can be ineffective and you can be out the door." This is a powerful concept. If you, as a young woman, can recalibrate and adjust to the reality that not everyone is going to be your friend, conflicts will feel less personal.

That said, people-pleasing is a hard pattern to break, because getting other women to like us is often how we operate at the office and in life. As any woman knows, information sharing is a powerful way of integrating yourself into a social group, and the office is no exception. Casey, 26, whose her first job was at a public relations company in Los Angeles, says the wool was pulled over her eyes because she was too eager to get her female co-workers to like her. "They were all young women around my age. We would all laugh and have lunch together and I would try to bond with them." Casey discovered pretty fast that she was too trusting. "The girls who I thought were my friends were actually sabotag-

ing me behind my back, telling my bosses bad things about me."
After that experience, she learned to put up a bit of armor, even if
everyone seems really "nice and friendly."

Dede Bartlett, a former vice president at Altria Group, Inc.,
advises young women to "slowly build *a bank account of trust and
credit* at the office." Trust is something that builds over time, so
you can't expect to start a new job and automatically trust your
coworkers—or have them trust you. Think back to the professional behaviors presented in chapter 2 and don't start spilling
your deep, dark secrets all at once.

Co-worker? BFF? Acquaintance?
Reading Between the Blurry Lines

As we all know, the workday can feel like a drag without office
camaraderie. It's the office friendships, the people you go out to
shop with at lunch or grab coffee with in the middle of those seemingly endless days, that make it all a little more fun. As Heather,
a software engineer, puts it, "The day gets pretty long without that
kind of support network." Just be aware of how far you take it.

Sonya Lockett agrees, with one caveat: "You can have friendly
relationships with people, but the bottom line is that it is work. "

Lockett touches on an important point. It's not necessarily
healthy, or good for your job, to have friendship expectations of
the people who may end up being your boss or who may be
responsible for making decisions about your future in the workplace. Of course you will have office friendships, but don't try to
fit everyone in that category. Rachel, a school administrator, started
her career working at a large university. When she announced

that she was leaving, her female boss became very distant. "She didn't speak to me for the rest of the five weeks before I left." Rachel's situation illustrates what happens to so many women at work. That is, women become friendly and blur the line between friend and co-worker. Although Rachel's boss felt betrayed and hurt that her employee was "leaving the nest," she infused too many of her personal, almost motherly, feelings into their professional relationship.

Phyllis Chesler, author of *Woman's Inhumanity to Woman*, writes that when we view other women as pseudo-family members, we run the risk of trusting female strangers more than we should. Many business and professional women have been blindsided by such expectations.[3]

It's this often subtle, but important, distinction between friends and friendliness that we need to be aware of. It's work, not a social club. Friendship is definitely not a prerequisite of effectively working together. Moreover, you certainly don't have to be best friends with everyone you work with. It's natural to want some personal connection in the workplace, and that's great. Just be aware about the parameters of these friendships.

The red flags of office friendships
Sometimes it's difficult to know what the parameters of a "normal" office friendship should be. Here are a few signs that your office friendship is teetering on the unprofessional.

- You spend more time socializing than working. A healthy (read: productive) professional relationship should be the other way around.

3. Phyllis Chesler, *Woman's Inhumanity to Woman*. New York: Thunder's Mouth Press, 2002, p. 14.

- The emotional energy you spend worrying about your office friendships has started to distract you from doing your job. It's the work, not your personal relationships, that should be consuming most of your time at the office.

- You constantly feel hurt, offended, and sidestepped by your female co-workers. If this is the case, you've probably become too emotionally invested in the relationship and need to create some distance.

Please, Don't Be Like This

Madeline Albright, the former and first female secretary of state famously said on a 2004 panel at Columbia University about eliminating violence and discrimination against women, "There is a special place in hell for women who don't help each other."[4] If women are ever going to create the kind of social capital that has existed between men for decades, we need to stop sabotaging one another.

Anne Fairfax, co-owner of the architecture firm Fairfax & Sammons, had an experience early in her career that illustrated quite poignantly the effects of not being helped by a woman who was in an opportune position to support her. "When I was young and working as a freelancer, I had designed this really beautiful bathroom, and one of the higher-ups in the firm asked another young, female employee who designed it. The other young woman, knowing full well that I had designed it, replied, 'Oh,

4. Lindsay Schubiner, "Female Leaders Discuss Sexism and Violence," *Columbia Daily Spectator*, September 24, 2004.

some freelancer.' I'll never forget how she wouldn't give me credit. And I swore that when I had my own firm that I wouldn't tolerate that kind of behavior. Just that one comment set me up in competition with her."

Probably the most pervasive and destructive form of dirty play among women is gossip. It's why Kathy Bonk of Communications Consortium Media Center has created a *no triangling rule* at her office. It's the idea that if someone has a problem, he/she should go directly to the person with whom he/she's having the problem, instead of going to a third party. This prevents "triangling"—or complaining to a third and oftentimes unrelated party. By employing this strategy, you'll help prevent those *Why is she being such a bitch?* moments and ultimately gain more respect from your co-workers and supervisors. Even though it might be hard to walk into your boss's office and give her direct feedback, it's better than telling someone else and having your boss hear it from a third party.

Along those same lines, setting a no-gossip policy for yourself will give you a good reputation around the office. Alexandra, 36, has worked in management positions at many large corporations and sets a firm rule about not becoming the *water cooler girl*. "In general, when I'm leading a team, I will state pretty clearly that if you have a problem, bring it directly to me. I set a baseline where it is known that gossip will not be a supported behavior. When I'm in a situation where people are gossiping, I try to remove myself from the situation." As a professional, you don't want to be gossiped about, so don't gossip about other people.

Working with Women of *All* Ages

With young women entering the workforce in unprecedented numbers, women in their twenties and thirties are working for women in their forties, fifties, and sixties. This often results in a generational culture clash, in which you may end up working for a female boss that is twenty or thirty years your senior, and who rose through the ranks in a very different workplace.

A May 2006 *Wall Street Journal* article on the topic of generational integration in the workplace, stated that there are now four generations of women together in the workplace—more than at any time in the past.[5] The article describes how these generational dynamics play out: "Some female bosses from Generation X (born between 1965 and 1980) are finding a clear generation gap with female employees from Gen Y (born after 1980). Likewise, some female bosses who are baby boomers (1946 to 1964) or from the World War II generation (born after 1945) often have trouble relating to women born at other times."[6]

Jean Otte, founder and CEO of Women Unlimited, says that one source of tension is that "young women don't value how much of a history there is with an older person." Young women today grew up with the protection of Title IX—the federal law that made sex discrimination in government programs illegal. It's why many women of other generations think Gen Y women see themselves as entitled. As one former executive from Liz Claiborne said in the *Wall Street Journal* article, "Today's twentysomethings were coddled as girls—chauffeured from play date to play date—and now want to be coddled on the job."[7]

5. Jeff Zaslow, "A New Generation Gap: Differences Emerge Among Women in the Workplace," *Wall Street Journal*, May 4, 2006.
6. Ibid.
7. Ibid.

This has spawned a dynamic where just 53 percent of women said they "learn from older co-workers," according to a recent survey released by Randstad USA, an employment-services firm. And, according to the 2006 *Wall Street Journal* article, only 23 percent of women under age 34 said older co-workers energize them and bring new ideas to the table.[8] That's why women of Gen Y need to start thinking about how to work more effectively and productively not only with women in their peer group, but with the women who came up in the ranks before them. With such a variety of age groups in the twenty-first-century workplace, it's essential to maximize what you can learn from *all* of your female co-workers.

Wende Jager Hyman, the executive director of the Woodhull Institute, a leadership and training program for women, attributes women's workplace ruts to what she has coined the *psychology of scarcity*. "Women have developed a psychology of scarcity. The psychology is that there isn't going to be enough room for two of us. That, unfortunately, has led to a dearth of mentors, but, remember, there are never too many fabulous female attorneys, doctors, or engineers." Arya, a consultant, observes how this psychology of scarcity plays out, particularly if you are a woman *and* a minority. "You think to yourself, 'Since there are so few women and so few minorities, that whoever comes in is going to come in and push me out of the way.'"

Amber, who runs her own business, pinpoints a universal truth: "It is hard to get older and see younger women. You think to yourself, 'I can't believe she has accomplished more than I have.' I do my best to overcome that. But you want to think of yourself as a rock star." That's true. However, that doesn't mean you should fear that the arrival of a New Girl will undermine your

8. Ibid.

position, or write off the older women you work with as out of touch. There is room for all of us.

One effective strategy to help foster camaraderie with a female boss or older co-workers is just as simple as: Help her do her job to the best of her ability. Dede Bartlett advises, "Ask your boss on a regular basis if there is anything more you can do to help her. Think along the lines of *what can I do to make you look good.*" Amy Dorn Kopelan, a former senior executive at ABC, and president of Coach Me, Inc., echoes this advice. "Your job is to make your boss look good. If, as a woman leader, I realize that you know that you have come on board to make me look good, I'm going to rely on you more." This strategy might help diffuse some of the "I struggled and so should you" attitude.

But it is also incumbent on these top achievers to reach out to young women and recommend the up-and-comers for promotions. If you work for a woman who isn't doing this, Kopelan suggests that you get out. "There will be catty women, but you have to work for a woman who is championing you. If that is not the case, you have to think about going elsewhere."

While doing everything you can to make your female boss look good is important, you can't forget about the relationships with the women at your level. There is a lot of talk in business books and magazines these days about "managing up"—a fancy way of saying that you should focus on your relationship with your boss. What young women forget, particularly with their female co-workers, is managing laterally or down. Becky Newman of the University of California, San Diego, observes that a lot of young women manage up very well, but they aren't as worried about working with their colleagues. It's definitely important to please your boss and "manage up," but if you neglect to manage your relationships with your co-workers, and your female co-workers in particular, there is a problem.

The New Girls' Network

Building on the idea of managing down/laterally is a blueprint for how to help the next woman along. Olivia had her first job at an investment bank, and was lucky to find the kind of support that has the potential to make a New Girl's career. "Erin, who was just three years older than me, was unbelievably helpful. She was the epitome of noncompetitive. She would give me credit for the projects we worked on together. Most important, she would take the time to teach me everything." Olivia says that "Erin" imparted empowering advice to her. "Erin reinforced that I'm going to make valuable contributions. She really encouraged me to speak up." Now, think what the workplace would be like if we all had an *"Erin."* The idea of an "Erin" is really about taking your professional relationships with your peers to the next level. For instance, maybe your family friend is an administrator at a hospital, and your friend Jamie wants to get into hospital administration. Arrange a lunch meeting for the three of you.

It's based on the simple idea that you should be reaching out to women in your peer group. Think of it as a *New Girls' Network*—a network of young women who help each other climb the ladder. Imagine, for example, if you had access to a database of young women whom you could call on when you needed a favor or advice. Men have been doing it for decades—does *the Old Boys' Club* sound familiar?—and if you start now, think what a twenty-year edge on networking could do, not only for your career, but for the career of women everywhere.

A 2003 *New York Times* article, "How to Move Up? The Sorority Track," detailed how professional networking through college sororities has gained momentum in recent years, fueled by a rise in the number of women in management and professional positions who have influence over hiring—21.4 million in 2002 compared with 14.7 million a decade ago, according to the Labor Department.[9] That's worth restating: Over 20 million women have influence over hiring, and you certainly don't have to have been in a sorority to take advantage of this growing number of women in management positions. "Sororities are tapping into what guys have done for years that women also need to do," said Karen Chevalier, vice president for programs for Phi Beta Phi. "But it is only now that women are learning to use those connections."[10] All women, sorority sisters or not, have the ability to tap into this type of network—and benefit from it.

Gail Evans, author of *She Wins, You Win,* advocates a radical shift in our thinking about helping other women. "Women need to start thinking that for every one woman who succeeds, I succeed a little and for every woman who fails, I fail a little. We need to get on the same team, which is something we haven't done yet."[11] As many have pointed out, imagine the impact women could have if they bonded together to create change at work. The bottom line is that it is in our best interest to help other women succeed.

Judy Rosener, a columnist for the *Orange County Business Journal,* writes, "Male networks, often first based on personal

9. Ruth La Ferla, "How to Move Up? The Sorority Track," *New York Times,* July 13, 2003.
10. Ibid.
11. CNN Live Saturday, "Dollar Signs: Women in Business," aired November 15, 2003.

relationships, produce career advancement. Female organizations, often first based on career advancement, produce personal relationships. Women often form friendships in networks, and end up using the network merely for moral support instead of fulfilling professional goals. Always remember the purpose of a network."[12] A critical point here. It's not just about "helping" other women in the spirit of altruism. It's about creating a culture where women assist each other in advancing to higher positions.

12. Quoted in Sarah Kaip, "The 'Old Boy' Network," *Women's Media*. www. womensmedia.com/new/Old-Boy-Network.shtml

TAKEAWAYS

- Don't triangle. If you are having a problem with your co-worker or boss, don't complain to a third person (i.e., create a triangle). Instead, talk directly to the person with whom you're having the conflict.

- Don't view the other women you work with as family. They aren't your mother, sister, or aunt. Even if there are surface similarities, these are professional relationships, and viewing female co-workers as family members is just not professional.

- You can be friendly without being friends. Friendship is not a prerequisite to working together.

- Don't try to be a people pleaser. Attempting to get all of your co-workers to like you has few, if any, professional benefits.

- Don't divulge too much personal information at first. Even if it seems as if you have a lot in common with your female co-workers, it takes time to figure out which people to trust. Think of it as slowly building up a bank account of trust and credit.

- Confront problems as they arise. If you let problems

with co-workers fester, you are going more likely to triangle, feel resentful, and gossip.

- If you work for a woman, make sure she knows it's your priority to make her look good.

- Don't assume women of a different generation are "out of touch." Reach out to them, and be an active part of trying to bridge the generational divide. It's definitely to your benefit.

- Foster relationships with women of your own peer group.

- Build the New Girls' Network by bringing the next woman along.

CHAPTER EIGHT

Making Sense of Mixed Signals and Stereotypes
Be Assertive, Not Aggressive (or, She's Just a Detail-Oriented Perfectionist)

There's no doubt about it, workplace behavior cues are often confusing. On one hand, you want to be assertive, but you don't want to be aggressive. You want to come off as collegial and easy to get along with, but not be a total pushover.

So how the heck do you find the middle ground? Dana, the construction manager, like many young women, finds the challenge is to assert yourself without being nasty. Deborah Tannen, an authority on gender issues at work, and author of *Talking from 9 to 5*, when interviewed for a 2003 article about women's advancement, observed that men state their opinions as fact, especially when they're in leadership roles. "If a woman does it, she's perceived as aggressive, pushy, and non-feminine. But then if she tries to meet expectations of how a woman should talk, she's perceived as soft and ineffectual. It's a double-blind."[1]

It's the question that perplexes most women in the workplace:

1. Gene Epstein, "More Women Advance, but Sexism Persists," *College Journal*, June 5, 2003.

How do you set boundaries without alienating your co-workers? There are no hard-and-fast rules about what this fine line is, but there are situations that illustrate how these things *actually* play out at the office. Jennifer Baumgardner, author of *Manifesta*, used to supervise a team of interns at *Ms.* magazine, and recalls an intern who took it upon herself to phone singer-song writer Tori Amos's agent and set up an interview. "I ended up shooting her initiative down because I wasn't sure an intern should do the interview, despite her tremendous go-getter spirit."

As Baumgardner's intern learned, taking initiative is great, but you probably don't want to take on a high-profile task, such as calling important clients or setting up meetings, without first running it by your boss. Baumgardner said that she would have been more open to the idea if her intern had scoped out the situation with her, before calling Tori Amos's agent.

Mary, 22, a government employee, found that figuring out the distinction between aggressive and assertive is a craft, and one worth mastering. Mary worked with a woman whose manner was hostile and aggressive. "When I saw her name on my e-mail screen, my blood pressure would rise. If she had been polite and easy to deal with, I would have been more likely to help her." Everyone wants to work with people who are pleasant. There are, of course, going to be times when you need to be tough, but in Mary's situation, her co-worker's outwardly aggressive demeanor ultimately made her less effective. The takeaway: Not every work situation is going to require you to play hardball, so adjust your aggressiveness on a case-by-case basis.

Caroline Baum, of Bloomberg News, cautions that you can be too forceful. "I think you can come on too strong and turn off people. That would be true of men, too. Aggressive, in my mind, is pushy. It is pushy to stick your nose into where it shouldn't be. For example, I had a friend who was on a great news story and someone stole it from her. That is aggressive and also sort of rotten."

Lisa Witter, general manager of Fenton Communications, encourages young women to think of how they assert themselves at the office as being like driving a car with five speeds. You have to know instinctively when to ride in gear five and when to shift down to gear two. Basically, you have to calibrate your speed to different terrain. "I think the challenge of the modern business world is to be a bulldog without looking like a bulldog. The key to being aggressive is also to be gracious and to be a good listener. I see a lot of times that young people come in at fifth gear and they really should be at second gear and everyone is looking at them like, what are you doing?" So it's really not an either/or proposition. It's just figuring out, situation by situation, which gear you need to be in. Like the rest of your New Girl education, there is going to be a learning curve as you figure out what gear is most comfortable and appropriate for each situation, and you'll figure that out by trial and error.

Shocking! Being Likeable Wins at Work

Having a good relationship with your co-workers could be one of the strongest assets an employee, man or woman, brings to the workplace. A growing body of research has found that likable employees may actually have more success on the job. A 2005 study in the *Harvard Business Review*, as reported in a December 2005 *USA Today* article, found that personal feelings toward an employee play a more important role in forming work relationships than is commonly acknowledged. It is even more important than how competent an employee is perceived to be.[2]

While being a pushover or being "too nice" is definitely not ideal, neither is being rude or unpleasant. In fact, nearly 60 percent of consumers said that, when faced with rudeness, they take their business elsewhere, even if it means going out of their way or paying a higher price, according to a 2002 survey by Eticon, a Columbia, South Carolina–based consulting firm.[3]

Statistics and studies clearly reveal that being respectful is an effective business strategy, particularly when it comes to interacting with clients. For example, if your boss sees that you interact well with clients, co-workers, customers, and business vendors, he/she is more likely to hand over responsibility in that arena.

Self-Promote—Because No One Else Is Going to Do It for You

Still, being likeable doesn't mean that you should be a wallflower, as a group of 177 women—all part of a professional association called "100 Women in Hedge Funds"—learned at a workshop they attended. It was profiled in a 2003 *New York Times* article where the attendees were described by one attendee as the "best and brightest" in a business that is hardly for the timid.[4] The workshop focused on what many workplace experts have noticed most women fall short on—self-promotion. The workshop started

2. Stephanie Armour, "Another Reason to be Nice: It'll get you far on the job," *USA Today,* December 28, 2005.
3. Eticon (press release), "Study Measures Impact of Rudeness and Respect in Business." Columbia, SC, June 6, 2002. www.eticon.com/2002_survey.pdf
4. Ellen Rapp, "Executive Life; A Pep Talk for Women to End All Pep Talks," *New York Times*, September 28, 2003.

off with Peggy Klaus, a leadership and communication coach, asking the participants to pair off and tell each other three things they were proud of. Klaus observed that some of the women looked as if "they'd rather be having a root canal."[5]

Klaus asked her audience what the word "brag" brought to mind. The responses included "selfish," blowhard," "know-it-all" and "insecure." One woman participating in the conference commented, "I acted like I wasn't important. By not being able to communicate how I could add value to the organization, I lost respect and power."[6]

One Wall Street professional who was passed over for a promotion to managing director sought Klaus's services. She was coached on the art of self-promotion, and wrote down her accomplishments and presented them to her boss. She was subsequently promoted.[7]

But self-promotion isn't easy, and is not something young women are taught much about. It's a rare college or graduate school that has a class on self-promotion, yet it's a critical skill to master. Essie Chambers, executive director of development at Noggin, believes that self-promotion is about recognizing your strengths. "I realized that I had a knack for certain management parts of the job, but I was strong in the creative part. In self-promoting, I tried to articulate how I could bring both of those particular strengths to the job. I think, too, if you are going to self-promote, you have to be honest about your weaknesses. Women often project the whole 'I'm in control attitude.' I always own my mistakes. I can be self-deprecating as much as I can be self-

5. Ibid.
6. Ibid.
7. Ibid.

promoting. Any time I speak publicly, I always give an anecdote about how I failed five times before I succeeded."

Self-promotion, however, isn't just about piping up when things go well; it's also about speaking up when they don't. Suzanne, 31, a consultant in Chicago, has learned that it is absolutely imperative to assert yourself when you get negative feedback. "At my company, after each project, you are given an evaluation. I worked on this one project where I got a really bad evaluation. Instead of just letting it go, I printed out a whole packet of everything I had done and put it together to present to the guy who gave me the bad evaluation. He ended up changing my evaluation. With that new evaluation I was ranked much higher, and a few months later I was promoted. I think in the end, too, I earned a lot of respect." It was after this incident that Suzanne had that critical "Aha!" moment, where she realized that no one was going to speak up for her—it's an epiphany every young woman needs to have.

Jackie, a child psychologist in Chicago, wasn't assertive about defining the parameters of her job and her supervisor kept piling on more work. "I went to her and said, 'I want to do the best job I can.' My boss said that she respected me for being honest and setting limits about the amount of work I could take." Jackie believes her boss responded so well to her approach because of how she broached the topic. "If I had been aggressive about it, I wouldn't have opened up a dialogue."

Tory Johnson, CEO of Women for Hire and career expert for ABC's *Good Morning America*, also advises young women who are new on the job to speak up and share ideas. "So often, young people think that they can't be taken seriously. Don't be afraid. Just because you are the new girl on the job doesn't mean that it's your place to be quiet. You are going to have a lot of missed opportunities if you don't assert yourself." Think of it this way: Employers hire people because they want value-added comments, suggestions, and ideas, not a wallflower.

You Are Worth It

Another area where it is critical to be assertive or even (*gasp!*) aggressive, is when it comes to salary negotiation. Michelle, 27, a researcher at a nonprofit in New York, sees this as a pervasive problem among New Girls. "I think young women don't believe they are worth as much as they are, and people take advantage of that. I didn't negotiate my salary. I know a lot of young women and my peers feel this way and say, 'They will give me a raise if I deserve it.' " It's what Carol Frohlinger and Deborah Kolb, the founders of Negotiating Women, Inc., coined the term *tiara syndrome* to describe. Frohlinger says it's when you keep your head down and do your work and expect that someone will notice you and place a tiara on your head. "That never happens. Everyone in the corporate world is focused on themselves."

When Brittany, the head of communications for a well-known art exhibit, was promoted and asked to take over the job of another employee, she was hesitant to ask for a raise. Brittany is emblematic of what could well be an epidemic among young women who don't ask for raises or negotiate their salary.

Wende Jager Hyman of the Woodhull Institute says that when you don't negotiate your salary, people will perceive you as not having a backbone. "You have to say, 'I know this is what I can add to the bottom line.' I counseled one young woman and she got a raise just because of the way she presented herself during the salary negotiations. The company was extremely impressed because they saw how that was going to translate into how she would interact with clients." In other words, this young woman's poise, firmness, and willingness to take a stand on an issue were all seen as assets by her employer.

Lisa Witter, who does a lot of hiring for Fenton Communications, sees young women neglecting salary negotiation left and right. "With every job offer I've made the men were more aggressive about how much money they asked for. The men just come in and say, 'This is what I need to make.' Women usually respond by saying 'somewhere between here and there.' They don't put a line in the sand. It really sets a different tone in terms of their self-confidence. I think the single most important thing for a young woman to project coming into the workforce is self-confidence."

The good news is that learning to negotiate your salary or a raise is not rocket science. But, like anything, there are techniques and strategies to being effective at it. Suzanne, the consultant, found that one of the biggest challenges was learning that she could negotiate her salary. "I was just grateful to have a job. But I ended up losing out because of that mentality. When I left for business school, I was making much less than my male colleagues. The guy I worked with was making forty thousand more than me, and I even have a graduate degree!"

Statistics certainly reflect this inequity. A 2003 study of thirty-eight business students, by Lisa A. Barron, an assistant professor of organizational behavior at the Graduate School of Management at the University of California at Irvine, found that 85 percent of the men but only 17 percent of the women felt that it was up to them to make sure the company paid them what they were worth; the rest felt that their worth would be determined by what the company paid them.[8] The economic repercussions of not negotiating your first salary are staggering. According to Linda Babcock and Sara Laschever, authors of *Women Don't Ask: Negotiation and the Gender Divide*, it was calculated that just by not negotiating on a first job offer and simply accepting what she is offered, a woman stands to lose more than half a million dollars by age 60. Men are four times as likely to negotiate on a first salary, which sets a baseline for your future earning potential.[9]

A Salary Negotiation Script

The first couple of times you negotiate for your salary, it may be intimidating. To help get you over the first few hurdles, here's a script of how you can start making what you are worth.

- **Start positive.** Career expert Tory Johnson advises young women to begin the negotiation process by saying something along the lines of, "I'm thrilled by the offer, but I would like to get the whole compensation package that you have offered me in writing."

- **Be firm.** If they end up offering something lower than what you expected, say something like, "I appreciate the offer, but I have to say that the base salary is less (or significantly less) than I anticipated, given what the appropriate range is for this position and for the skills and experience that I bring to the position. Can

8. Abby Ellin, "When It Comes to Salary, Many Women Don't Push," *New York Times*, February 29, 2004.
9. Women Don't Ask: Negotiation and the Gender Divide, "A Conversation with Linda Babcock and Sara Laschever." www.womendontask.com/question.html

you give me a sense of how much room there is to
maneuver on this number?"

- **Find other points of negotiation.** If they still don't
budge on the number, have them agree to a salary
negotiation, or review, in six months as opposed to a
year. Even if you only get them to agree to that, you
have still negotiated!

Another crucial component of "the script" is doing your
homework. Carol Frohlinger suggests that young women research
what the prevailing market rate is for that job. There are many
career sites, such as Monster.com or Salary.com, which can lead
you to this valuable information. Frohlinger also suggests identifying any special expertise you have that might give you a little
more leverage, or put you in the upper tier of the pay bracket. For
example, maybe you've had a lot of internships and client contact
in the health-care field. Or, maybe you have won a writing fellow-
ship or another award that lends you some additional expertise,
thus giving you an edge over the competition. Whatever it is,
make sure your employer is aware of your assets, because that
can often mean a larger paycheck.

Frohlinger cautions young women to think about more than
the dollar signs, particularly if you are having a hard time getting
your employer to budge on his/her offer. In such situations, she
advises finding other parts of the job that might have more flexibility. For example, maybe you can negotiate to work on a specific
project, or with a certain group of clients. If it's congruent with the
culture at your office, you might even be able to negotiate another
week of vacation.

Neda, a freelance writer, says that when she first started working she thought it was taboo to discuss salary. "Especially coming out of an academic environment, where you get your due by what you give, the whole salary negotiating thing can be overwhelming." Neda quickly realized that she didn't want to continue working as a cocktail waitress to supplement her income. "I sat down with my boss and told him, 'Here is why it is difficult to be here with so little money.' People aren't going to say to you, 'Maybe we should be paying you more money.' I've learned to be pretty blunt. While my company couldn't raise my salary that much, I was able to negotiate a better title. 'Intern' and 'fellow' are nebulous terms, so I negotiated with them to have the title of 'editorial assistant,' which gave me a lot more leverage in the job market. It also really taught me that I should have talked about compensation when I first signed on."

To recap, here are some critical salary negotiation tips, courtesy of career expert Tory Johnson.

- **Bosses expect you to negotiate.** Remember that negotiation is a normal part of the hiring process.

- **Find out where your salary falls in the range for your industry.** For instance, is it between $25K and $35K, or $125K and $150K? You can't ask how much Kelly or Richard makes, but you can ask where your salary falls in the general range. Johnson says that most employers will give you some explanation. "For example, they might say it's at the lower end of the spectrum because you don't have that much experience, or they might say it's at the high end because of your GPA." Either way, it's helpful to know where you fall.

- **It's just business.** Don't think that if you ask for too much they aren't going to like you. It's not about someone liking you or not. It's about getting the fairest compensation for the work you are doing. Along those same lines, don't make it about how you need the money to maintain a certain standard of living, pay off student loans, or your mortgage.

- **Address your benefits.** Find out how much an employer will deduct, if anything, from your paycheck for health insurance. Some companies pay 100 percent of their employee's health insurance, while others do not. You need to understand what things are going to cost you. And while retirement might be the last thing on your mind, don't gloss over your 401k. Find out if your company has a retirement plan, and research the plan to decide if it's the best choice for you. If your company does not have a retirement plan, or if you are unhappy with the plan they offer, you might consider looking into IRA's (individual retirement plans).

Negotiating for a Raise

While negotiating your salary at the beginning of every new job is absolutely crucial—it sets the base for your future earning potential—negotiation is a perennial activity. The average raise is about 3.5 percent, which means some people get more, others receive less. Companies also vary in how they give raises. A raise is not a given; what you expect or ask for should be based on your performance and the company's performance. Oftentimes, all employees receive a standard small raise unless there is a serious performance issue. However, if you're hoping for a substantial raise, be aware that it's usually accompanied by a promotion.

To ensure you get the best raise and/or a promotion, Frohlinger advises that you keep an office journal. At the end of each month, note your contribution to projects, even if it's something as simple as the impact that rearranging the filing system had on office efficiency, or bigger things like the accolades you got from clients on your presentation. That way, at your end-of-year review, you can have a concrete list of things you have accomplished. It will also help circumvent the inventible agony you will go through when you have to write your review and you can't remember what you've done all year.

The Work Martyr Syndrome

The following might be something you've heard at work: Oh, that's Sally—she's really organized and has neat handwriting. That's Jane—she's really friendly on the phone. Or that's Megan—she is usually the last one to leave the office. It all sounds relatively benign, right? Think again. While on the surface these are innocent and even complimentary remarks, getting pigeonholed into these "administrative" categories can mean stagnation on the career ladder for young women, if they aren't careful.

Essie Chambers of Noggin calls this being a *work martyr*. Unfortunately, as she points out, it's a situation that young, single women often find themselves in: "I see young women working themselves to the bone." What Chambers correctly diagnoses is way beyond just working hard. It's when you are staying two or three hours later than everyone else at your level, taking on extra work, and sacrificing your health and sanity for no good reason except to prove that you can do the work. Being a work martyr has actually reached systemic levels. In a recent survey, 39 percent of women said they won't leave work if co-workers are still there burning the midnight oil.[10]

Although it might sound counterintuitive, being a work martyr might actually be impeding your success, not advancing it. By staying late at the office, skipping meals, and working weekends, you are decreasing your productivity and energy, not increasing it.

What fuels this Work Martyr Syndrome? For many young women, it's the belief that they are expendable, so they work twice as hard to prove otherwise. You aren't expendable! Repeat: You have valuable skills and assets that only *you* bring to the job.

But how do you know if you are a work martyr, or are just working really hard? Here are some telltale signs that you've become a martyr:

- You stay two to three hours later than everyone else on the same level at least a couple of times per week.

10. *Self* magazine, April 2005.

- You are coming in to work on the weekends or taking work home with you when no one else is.

- You are skipping meals, not getting sleep, and generally seeing a severe deterioration in your physical and mental health as a result of work.

- Your boss constantly singles you out to take on extra work.

- You can't remember the last time you had a lunch break.

- You haven't spoken to your friends and family in weeks.

- You slept underneath your desk last night.

- You've taken on so many extra responsibilities that you can't do your own job well.

Perfection: the inner demon of a NGOTJ

Work Martyr Syndrome is actually an outgrowth of another common trait of the New Girl—being a perfectionist. Lee Anne Bell, Ed.D., notes that women are more likely to define competence as perfection and are often guided by standards that are unnecessarily high.

Take Whitney, who now works in the research department of a financial services firm but whose first job was as a paralegal. Like so many young women, Whitney equates professionalism with perfection. "Being perfect is what it means to be professional. I found that at my job, girls were better paralegals. Girls are just more meticulous." Whitney puts a lot of pressure on herself to be perfect, and she's not alone. When asked about the key assets they brought to their jobs, most of the women interviewed for this book had similar answers: being a hard worker, and being a perfectionist.

While being detail oriented and wanting to get everything just right is important, there is a dark side: perfection can actually be a roadblock to getting ahead. In a 2003 *New York Times* article about workplace productivity, Annick Baudot-Moheg, an employee of Adobe Systems, presented a good solution: She talked about how she focuses only on details of projects that are relevant to her, rather than trying to do other people's work for them. As a result, she estimates that her productivity increased by about 50 percent.[11]

Perfectionists, take heed: No matter how careful you are, there will be times when things go wrong. It's the nature of the job, and a lesson that every employee—from assistants up to CEOs—learns quickly. For example, cosmetics executive Bobbi Brown was on the way to do the makeup for the governor of New Jersey and realized that she had left her makeup bag—everything she needed to complete the job—at home. By the time she discovered her mistake it was too late to turn back. "Instead of panicking and freaking out, I called a department store and I was able to improvise. If there had not been a department store nearby, I would have gone to the drugstore. You have to learn to roll with the punches and not be perfect."

Lorraine Lafferty, coauthor of *Perfectionism: A Sure Cure for*

---

11. Laura Koss Feder, "Personal Business; Slowing Down the Treadmill, with Help," *New York Times*, June 29, 2003.

Happiness, notes that perfectionists equate their self-worth with flawless performance. So they often dwell on trivial details and devote too much time to projects, which slows productivity. Sound familiar? Lafferty's advice is to *unperfect* it. She says that perfectionists need to realize that not everything on their desk is equally important. "Prioritizing what needs extra attention and what doesn't will make your workload and your stress levels more manageable.[12]

Also, keep in mind when you obsess over perfection, you miss the *real* priorities. Many young women said they became so over-whelmed and overloaded by the details of their projects that they weren't able to focus on the real priorities. Lizzie, 24, a junior employee at a branding firm in Chicago, fell into this trap. "I would double check the FedEx box one hundred times. What I should have been doing was taking a step back and thinking about what *really* needed to be done. When I finally learned to do that, I was so much better at my job and I was more productive."

Amber, who runs her own business, learned that "getting things done" is a tradeoff. "You just need to get 80 percent of everything done." What Amber picked up on is a critical work-place lesson: To prioritize your tasks, you have to think about the bigger picture. There's a compromise between staying till mid-night and making sure everything looks perfect, and anticipating what tasks need to be accomplished in the coming days or weeks. Once you learn to make this distinction, you'll be able to priori-tize and ultimately be a more valuable employee.

---

12. Aviva Patz, "Who Needs Perfect? Why super high expectations may be harm-ing your health, relationships and career." www.lifetimetv.com/reallife/health/features/perfect2.html

How Not to Get Assistant-ized

Admittedly, it's hard *not* to get mired in the details, particularly when the details are your job, as is often the case during the beginning stages of your career.

When Caroline first started as an editorial assistant she was responsible for all the scheduling, answering the phones, and other administrative tasks. While she only occasionally received higher-level editorial assignments, she noticed that some of the male employees at her level got them more often. She recalls, "I definitely got pigeonholed into 'cute little Caroline can do this and that administrative task.'"

Kimberly had a similar experience when she worked as an assistant to a high-level executive. "At first, I was very eager to prove that I could take on more, and one of the things that I noticed [was] I was getting a lot of praise for being organized, cheerful, and sweet. One of the men I worked for praised me for answering the phone pleasantly and for organizing papers well." Caroline and Kimberly landed in a trap that so many New Girls fall into. That is, they were so adept at the "assistant" tasks that they were asked to take on more and more of them.

Martha Burk, a political psychologist and women's equity expert, advises young women to monitor themselves to avoid getting *assistant-ized*. "It's a rare boss that is going to come and say, 'You are focusing too much on the minutia.' Women have to say to themselves, 'What is the larger goal I want to accomplish here beyond the detail work? Do I want to be put on a certain assignment, and how is spell-checking the document for the tenth time going to help?'" Of course, there is an appropriate amount of time that everyone has to be in an assistant or entry-level position and learn the ropes. But as you move forward in your career, be cognizant of how long you spend in that position and whether it's congruent with the norm of your industry. For instance, in some professions people are assistants for years before they get promoted, and in others it's a six-month-to-a-year transition position.

Being a great assistant can also be a catch-22 because, while you want to do a good job, doing so could actually hinder you from moving up. Career expert Tory Johnson sees it happen quite often. "It's very easy for women to get stuck in support roles." To break out of the vicious cycle, Johnson advises young women to set a strict limit. "You have to be willing to say, 'I will do this for a certain amount of time,' depending on your industry. After a year or so, you become pegged and it's more difficult for your employer to see you in a different light." But even if you have gotten pegged, Johnson says it's not too late to break out of an assistant role. "You can say to your boss that you need to move, and you can create a strategy for career growth."

Kimberly found one way to break out of getting "assistant-ized" was to create opportunities. "When I worked at this large TV station, I wanted to practice being an anchor, and on the weekends they practiced with the B team and I was able to stand in and be the anchor. I was able to write and produce a little segment, and it became my demo. I found that it was a good way to show people that, while I was in an assistant position, I was also capable of executing bigger projects."

Myia, an up-and-coming executive who rose through the ranks very quickly—from an assistant to a manager of a full team—picked up a few key points along the way on how you can break out of the assistant track. "I know, in my industry, we are always looking for 'the next best thing.' So I made a point to be on a lookout for those things. Whether it was attending seminars, cutting out articles, or e-mailing my boss links, I always had my ear to the ground. It might seem like sucking up, but it shows people that you are capable of so much more."

Furthermore, staying in low-level positions for too long is what some, such as Ilene H. Lang, president of Catalyst, the leading research and advisory organization working with businesses and professionals to expand opportunities for women at work, attributes to the glaring absence of women at the top. In a December 2006 *New York Times* article, "How Suite It Isn't: A Dearth of Female Bosses," Lang says that women are almost two and half times as likely to be channeled into staff jobs like Human Resources and communications than into operating roles where they would be generating revenue and managing profit and loss." Lang's calculus is this: "When more women hold line positions, there will be more women top earners." That's why it's imperative not to get assistant-ized.[13]

Another good way to avoid getting assistant-ized is to think about how your task, no matter how small, fits into the larger scheme of your organization. Being the low woman on the totem pole means that you are going to be doing the occasional—or not so occasional—mundane task. But if you show interest in the task, or even suggest ways in which it can be done more effectively, it will demonstrate to your boss that you are thinking beyond your job—a quality employers want in people they promote.

13. Julie Creswell, "How Suite It Isn't: A Dearth of Female Bosses," *New York Times*, December 17, 2006.

Setting Boundaries

Speaking of assistants, how do you draw the line between your duties as a regular assistant and a personal assistant? This is a line that, as most assistants will tell you, gets quite blurry.

Brooke, 25, an assistant at a large luxury conglomerate, says that for her it's situational. "I don't mind waiting at my boss's house for a furniture delivery, but I do mind going to buy his girl-friends gifts. When I first started, he asked me to go to Victoria's Secret and buy lingerie for his girlfriend. I did it, but now I won't. It is one thing to help him move, but it's another to help pick out lingerie. It's really a personal comfort thing. But it's very difficult to tell your new boss that you don't want to do things that he is asking you to do."

Penelope Trunk, a career columnist for *Business 2.0* maga-zine, writes that people who let this happen frequently are seen as doormats, and they are often left on the ground floor.[14] If you don't want to buy lingerie for your boss, book airline tickets for his 20-year-old girlfriend, or blot grease from his fried chicken, you've really got to speak up. Doing these things once in a while is okay to get on your boss's good side, but if it becomes a pattern you will be seen as a doormat.

Amanda, 24, an assistant editor in New York, found that it's very easy to get taken advantage of as a young woman because you have that potent combination of being eager, young, help-ful, and capable. "I was definitely taken advantage of. One time, my boss's assistant was out of the office so I covered for her. My boss called and asked me to find an e-mail address. I looked and looked for it and couldn't find it, so I called her to

14. Penelope Trunk, "Tired of the Grease? Become a Squeaky Wheel. Why it may be time to speak up instead of sucking up." CNNMoney.com, February 1, 2003.

say that I just couldn't find it. She asked me, 'Did you check the garbage?' I then went through her garbage and, lo and behold, I found the e-mail address between a turkey sandwich and some crumpled tissues. It ended up just being the person's first and last name at AOL. *How could she not have remembered that?* I thought to myself. In retrospect, I think I could have said to her that I didn't feel comfortable picking through her garbage."

As any assistant will tell you, it's an extremely personal relationship you have with your boss. You probably know more about him/her than anyone else. In the best of cases, it's a relationship that helps your boss do his/her job better, and provides crucial training and a springboard to bigger and better things for the assistant. Still, you, as the assistant, have rights and can set some boundaries.

General Rules About Where to Draw the Line When You Are an Assistant

- Don't do anything that you wouldn't ask a friend to do for you.

- Don't do anything that might get you arrested (obviously).

- Don't do anything that, if other people at the firm found out about it, would get you fired.

- Don't do anything that you would feel weird telling your parents about.

- Don't do anything that compromises your integrity (e.g., help your boss cheat/lie to someone else even if that someone is his/her wife, child, etc.).

- Don't blur your personal time and your work time. You shouldn't be called on to do errands and/or discuss work 24/7.

Trying to decipher the mixed signals of what's expected of you at the office can be exhausting. But these are crucial workplace issues for you to be aware of, particularly when it comes to salary and raise negotiation, staying out of the work martyr trap, and understanding the difference between professionalism and perfectionism. Once you make sense of the mixed signals around you, you'll be a more efficient, valuable employee, the type of employee who is poised to move up the corporate ladder.

TAKEAWAYS

- You don't have to be a bitch to be assertive. It's all about how you say it. Tone is everything.

- You'll probably go through some trial-and-error as you figure out how much to assert yourself. Remember the car analogy: Sometimes you'll need to be in first gear and sometimes you'll need to be in fourth.

- No one is going to do it for you, so make a commitment to self-promote.

- Negotiate your salary. Women stand to lose hundreds of thousands of dollars over the course of their career by not negotiating their salary on their first few jobs—the jobs that set the pay scale for future earning potential.

- Remember that salary negotiation is a perennial activity. To give yourself the most leverage at your yearly review, keep a monthly log of tasks you are doing at the office so you aren't stumped for material when review time comes.

- Stop trying to do everything perfectly—it's counter-productive. Instead, focus on the real priorities of your job.

- Don't become a work martyr. If you are always the one "martyring," it's time for a reality check. It's fine to stay late if everyone else is staying to finish a project, but if you're there every night and everyone else leaves hours before you, it's time to go home.

- Don't get assistant-ized. Working as an assistant can be a great gateway, but don't let yourself get stuck on the assistant track. Set strict limits with yourself about how long you will stay in the position. Also, being an assistant doesn't mean that your boss has carte blanche to ask you to do anything. It's completely appropriate to set boundaries and limits.

CHAPTER NINE

Avoiding a Bad Breakup
When and How Do You Leave a Job . . . and How to Handle It When a Job Leaves You

Just as New Girls need techniques to survive and thrive on the job, they also need strategies and tools for how to quit a job or survive a layoff.

But I'm *So* Lucky to Have This Job

If you are thinking of quitting your job, you've probably said to yourself, "But I'm *so* lucky to have this job." You're not alone.

You very well might be lucky to have your job, but this mentality may keep you in a dead-end, underpaid, and low-level job for way too long. Wende Jager Hyman, executive director of the Woodhull Institute, calls this the *fear-based model,* a term describing why employees stay in jobs they'd rather leave for fear that they'll never find another one. Instead, think that there are a hundred other jobs that need *you.*

Jager Hyman also points out that it's usually a lot worse for your employer than for you when you leave a job. "It's the worst thing in the world [for an employer] to lose employees. The truth is that once you reach a certain level, it will cost them one year's salary to train and replace you."

Sonya Lockett, vice president of public affairs at BET, says the most important piece of advice she can give to young women about quitting is, "Don't be afraid to take risks. I think I'm successful and where I'm at today because I followed that advice." The takeaway: Quitting is a calculated risk, but a risk worth taking if you think it will ultimately get you to a better place in your career.

How do you know when it's time to quit your job? There is, unfortunately, no foolproof formula. But here are signs that your current job is hindering your climb up the ladder:

- **You haven't been promoted above your entry-level position.** If you keep getting passed over for a promotion, this is a sign that you should start looking for a job with a better trajectory for growth.

- **Your skills and talents aren't being utilized.** If you don't feel challenged by your job and aren't learning something new from it, it's time to move on.

- **You have a bad boss.** You work for the human incarnation of Cruella de Vil, and months of public humiliation has given way to constant indigestion.

- **You dread going back to work on Monday mornings.** If you feel this way week after week, perhaps you made the wrong choice and ended up in a place that just isn't a good fit.

- **You are given far more responsibility than your salary or job title reflects.** If you are working two or three jobs for the price of one, it's time to move to a job that will pay you for all three.

Essie Chambers, executive director of development at Noggin, quit her first job after she kept waking up with horrible stomachaches because of her bad boss. Reflecting on that period in her career, she said, "There is nothing worse than that feeling. There was an opportunity opening up at a really great experimental place. However, taking that job meant starting at a lower position. I decided to take a step back to take a step forward."

By staying in a job that makes you miserable or in which your skills and talents aren't utilized, you are losing precious months—or even years—that could be spent in a job for which you're better suited. Plus, think of all those wasted hours you spend complaining to your parents and friends, which could be used on more productive activities—like networking and revising your résumé. Contrary to popular belief, the first years on your career path should not be so miserable that they make you want to quit. There is a difference between paying your dues and working at a job you hate. If your current job isn't working out, there is no shame in saying that you have given it your best and moving on.

The truth of the matter is that if you're an unhappy employee, you aren't doing anyone a favor by sticking around. An article in a business journal reveals what we all know: Unhappy employees are not only less productive, but are also a drag on the productive employees around the office.[1]

A Few Words About Quitting

Quitting a job is a twenty-first-century workplace rite of passage. The days of retiring with a gold watch from the company that offered you your first job are long gone. Also, according to a 2004 Associated Press poll, people over thirty were more likely to say they were very satisfied with their jobs than twenty-somethings, who said their job is something they mainly do for money.[2] In other words, members of Gen Y are the least happily employed generation in the workplace, and the most likely to quit their job.

Luckily, we live in a time when job-hopping is not stigmatized. According to the Bureau of Labor Statistics, the average person now holds more than nine jobs between the ages of eighteen and thirty-four! Pamela Paul, a former associate editor of *American Demographics*, when asked about this finding, commented, "Earlier wisdom says if you switched jobs too many times, you were looked upon as undependable or flighty. Now if you don't, you are seen as inflexible and stodgy."[3]

But before you give your two weeks' notice, it's critical to think about *how* you are going to quit. Like all job-related issues, there is a professional way to do it. Peter Vogt, a career coach for Mon-

---

1. M. Steele Brown, "Happy Returns," *The Business Journal of Kansas City*, July 7, 2003

2. Gerri Willis, "How to Deal with 'You're Fired!'" *Money* magazine, April 16, 2004.

3. Karen S. Peterson, "The 'Dark Side' of 25," *USA Today*, September 10, 2001

ster.com, gives some cardinal rules for quitting without burning bridges.[4]

Resign in person

Your boss deserves to hear it from you face-to-face. You owe it to him/her to provide an in-person explanation of why you're leaving. Resigning via e-mail, phone, or by simply not showing up for work is unacceptable.

Be completely honest and apologetic

In the face of something stressful like resigning, you may be tempted to make up some sort of fictional excuse. Don't. Lies always come back to haunt you. The truth is critical here, as is contrition on your part. Don't make excuses. Just tell it like it is. Focus on both your feelings and your legitimate concerns.

Offer to stay until someone else can be hired

Keley Smith-Keller, director of the Career Development Center at the University of South Dakota, says there's a useful lesson in the story of a student she worked with who decided to leave a retail management job after just one week. "The student sat down with his manager and told him that he could see he was the wrong fit for the job," says Smith-Keller. "He said he didn't want to waste any more of the employer's resources and training dollars—that such a thing wouldn't be courteous. So he offered to stay an extra week so that the manager could find a replacement." But if you have another job lined up, two weeks is a perfectly acceptable amount of time to give your boss.

4. Peter Vogt, "Four Ways to Quit Your New Job." content.monstertrak.monster .com/resources/archive/onthejob/leavenow

The Letter of Resignation

A final nuts-and-bolts issue: the letter of resignation. Judi
Perkins, a career coach, says to keep it as brief as possible. It
should include:[5]

- A direct statement that you are leaving your current
  company

- Details on your last date of employment

- If you feel comfortable, a sentence or two about how
  you appreciate the opportunity to have been a part of
  the organization

The letter should *not* include:[6]

- Why you are leaving

- Where you are going

- What you will be doing in your new position

- How much you will be making when you get there

- How bad you feel about leaving (or conversely, how
  glad you are to be going!)

5. Judi Perkins, "How to Resign," Badbossolog.com, May 1, 2006.
6. Ibid.

Fired, Let Go, Axed, a Mutual Parting: No Matter What You Call It, It's Hard

It's every worker's fear: getting fired. Whether you are 22, 26, 28, 35, or 62, it's never pleasant. And while Larry King and Joe Torre both say its "the best thing that ever happened" to them, to a young person in the workforce, getting fired is—in a word—horrifying. Losing a job can happen to anyone. Companies downsize, bad hiring decisions are made, e-mails are sent to the wrong person, and managers don't know how to properly train new hires, which can result in a dreaded conversation that includes the dreaded statement, "we need to let you go."

Alexandra, a former vice president at an insurance company, lost her job due to corporate downsizing. Like many people who are let go, she took it as an indictment of her capabilities. "The consequence of that mentality led me to a tepid and timid job search. It made me feel grateful just to get a job. You have to realize, if this happens to you, that it has nothing to do with you. My advice in retrospect is not to take it personally."

An article on the subject from asktheheadhunter.com, "Getting Fired Is a State of Mind," makes the excellent point that being fired is only a subjective judgment of you, not an absolute, objective one. "One boss's fire is another boss's hire. If that sounds trite, it is nonetheless true. People tend to forget it when they're suddenly left hanging in the breeze."[7]

Lisa, 22, was fired from her first internship at a public relations firm. Now, more happily employed, she says that being fired was great because it motivated her to think about what she really

7. Nick Corcodilos, "Getting Fired Is a State of Mind." www.asktheheadhunter.com/hagettingfired.htm

wanted to do and landed her in her current job, where she uses her language skills as a native Russian speaker.

Like many new hires, Amanda was given an employee manual to read that detailed her company's rules on forwarding internal e-mails outside of the company. Instructed by Human Resources to just sign the sheet and read it later, she was not well acquainted with the company's e-mail policy. Amanda forwarded a friend an e-mail from her boss, making a seemingly innocuous comment that her boss was "being silly." She was fired for doing it, in a string of technology-related firings. The other firings, however, were blog-related. "I did everything I could to try to keep my job. I wrote my boss a long e-mail about how I loved my job. My boss read my apology letter and said she took it to heart, but told me that she felt like she could never trust me again. After Human Resources told me that it was my last day, I said to my boss, 'Darlene, thank you for this opportunity.' I think it's important to end it on a good note. But after that I definitely felt like a failure. Here I was at entry level—supposedly the easiest position—and I had been fired. I felt like it was going to be so hard for me to find another job."

In the aftermath, Amanda got right back on her horse. "I took the weekend to collect myself and, that Monday morning, I was job searching. I ended up getting five job offers. But I definitely learned a lot. I don't send personal e-mails anymore, and I am a lot more careful about my Web usage. My advice to anyone who gets fired is that you have to take responsibility for what went wrong. And then move on. It's never all your fault." As Amanda's experience illustrates, there is always a confluence of factors that contribute to getting fired. The lesson to glean from this example is: Know thy company's technology/blog policies.

Although, it's almost a cliché to be the kid who gets fired for blogging, if you have a blog and don't want to get into a sticky situation, get a handle on your company's policy. A 2006 *New York Times* article on this topic quoted Alfred C. Frawley III, director of the intellectual property practice group at the law firm Preti Flaherty in Portland, Maine. "While there are differences in laws among jurisdictions, from a legal perspective, it is generally accepted that companies have the right to impose controls on their employees' use of computers and other equipment used for communication. As for content—information generated within a company—the law also allows employers to set limits, even on airing the company laundry outside the office, he said. Private employees do not receive the protection of the First Amendment because there is no government action involved. If an employee deviates from the policy, it may be grounds for termination."[8]

While the law may be defined, the Society for Human Resources Management found that, as of 2005, only 8 percent of the 404 human resource professionals it polled had blogging policies, whereas 85 percent did not—the other 7 percent did not know.[9] If you have a blog, or plan on blogging about your job, find out about your company's policy.

Now What?

So, you've weathered the worst of it—the actual firing. Now you have to address some logistical things. In the immediate aftermath of losing your job, you should review your contract (if you have

8. Anna Bahney, "Interns? No Bloggers Need Apply," *New York Times*, May 25, 2006.
9. Ibid.

one) or the employee handbook to see what it says about termination. Steven Mitchell Sack, employment attorney and author of the book *Getting Fired,* advises people to take the time to gather copies of their work and important documents, especially letters of recommendation, special notices of awards or promotions, and their personal lists of contacts and phone numbers.[10]

Most important, you want to make sure that you have health benefits. Some companies continue to pay your health insurance as part of your severance. The more probable scenario is that you will be able to continue with your old group coverage under COBRA, the Consolidated Omnibus Reconciliation Act, as long as your company employed twenty or more people. Under this plan, you will pay your company directly the amount of your health insurance premium. But COBRA isn't cheap. Individual coverage can cost as much as $400 a month and only lasts up to eighteen months.

Also, unemployment insurance is critical. To qualify for unemployment benefits, you need to prove you've been terminated. Don't think your boss is doing you any favors by calling your layoff a resignation. Make sure you get a letter confirming that you can claim unemployment. You can even apply online at www.dol.gov.

And finally, references . . . To avoid lawsuits, most companies will just verify your dates of employment and salary to a potential employer. However, if you ask for them to provide more information, they probably will. Just make sure they are details you would want said to a future employer. It's also polite and professional to ask a person if he or she will provide a reference; don't list that person as a reference without his/her knowing about it, especially if the parting wasn't mutual.

10. Willis, "How to Deal with 'You're Fired!' "

How Do You Explain Getting Fired
to Potential Employers?

You've figured out your health and unemployment insurance, and now you are back on your feet, looking for jobs and going on interviews. But how do you respond to your interviewer when he/she asks, "Why did you leave your last job?" It's a difficult question to answer, but in good old-fashioned public relations terms, you want to put the first "spin" on it. In other words, you want to have the first word on the issue. That's why Paul Barada, Monster.com salary negotiation expert, advises that honesty is the best policy when it comes to revealing you were fired. "The worst thing any job seeker can do is to be less than honest about the reason for leaving an employer and then have somebody check your references and discover you lied. That's a sure ticket to the unemployment office."

Getting fired is not the real atrocity; not learning from it is. In fact, explaining it to a prospective employer can actually provide a golden opportunity for you to articulate what you learned and how that will make you a better employee. In doing so, you'll come off as someone who can learn from her mistakes and take the best from situations. J. K. Rowling, Lance Armstrong, and New York mayor Michael Bloomberg were all fired before they reached the top of their fields.

Harry Potter creator Rowling lost her job as a secretary because she was caught writing creative stories on her computer. In a legendary move, she used her severance to write the first Harry Potter book. Today she is richer than the queen of England.

Lance Armstrong was fired from the French racing team in 1997, after he began cancer treatment. He went on to win the Tour de France.

Mayor Bloomberg was fired in 1981 after the company he was working for was acquired. Bloomberg used his stake in the company to start his own company, a venture that would revolutionize the way that Wall Street does business.[11]

As demoralizing or ego-deflating as getting fired or quitting a job may appear, it's never as bad as it seems. Not convinced? An entire book was written on this topic by Harvey Mackay, called *We Got Fired . . . and It's the Best Thing That Ever Happened to Us*. Even if you quit a job after six months, get fired after nine months, or downsized after five years, don't let that one event define who you are in your career. After you take the requisite mourning period, use it as a springboard to move onto the next bigger and better thing.

11. From Mayor Michael Bloomberg's biography. www.nyc.gov/portal/site/nycgov

TAKEAWAYS

- It's okay to quit your job if it's giving you ulcers, or it's just not the right match. No matter what the circumstances, try to exit gracefully and follow Peter Vogt's cardinal rules of quitting.

- Don't get caught in the fear-based model that you'll never find another job, because it's just not true. You got one job, you'll get another.

- Getting fired is not the end of the world, but make sure you leave with a fair severance package and a plan for continuing your health care.

- Also, establish how your old employer will handle references calls from future employers.

- Don't be risk averse. To find the right job, sometimes it's worth taking a step back to move forward.

CHAPTER TEN

The Future of Young Women at Work
How We Can Make It and Shape It

Gloria Feldt, the former president of Planned Parenthood and a longtime feminist activist, says her rallying cry to young women is, "Take over the workplace!"

It's why some have called for the second revolution in the workforce. In 2005 freelance writer Georgie Binks wrote about the face of the second revolution: "The first revolution came thirty-plus years ago when women entered the workforce. Now it's time for the second revolution—it's time the workforce changed for women and it looks like it might be happening."[1] The question that looms large, however, are: Will young women stay around long enough in the workforce for companies and individual managers and employers, to even see our value-added contributions? And furthermore, what are the real reasons behind why women leave the workplace and don't make it to the executive suite?

Barbara Annis, work place gender specialist and author of

---

1. Georgie Binks, "If you want to win women back, you have to start figuring out how they want to play the game," *CBC News ViewPoint*, February 25, 2005. www.cbc.ca/news/viewpoint/vp_binks/20050225.html

Same Words, Different Language, says the biggest myth about women leaving the workplace is that they do it because of work–life issues. As she persuasively argues, work–life balance is a universal issue. "Everybody is confronted with those issues, male or female. They [women] leave because they don't feel their own authentic strengths are valued. When we conduct exit interviews of female executives, they go to the competition, start their own businesses or go to a different industry . . . You want to work in a place that hasn't just allowed you in, but where you feel like you are contributing and making a difference."[2]

Courtney Martin, author of *Perfect Girls, Starving Daughters*, wrote about this phenomenon in a 2006 *Christian Science Monitor* article. Martin argues that the young women of Gen Y aren't opting out of work, they are opting out of the *traditional* workforce because they've found it to be unsatisfying, stifling, and unrewarding. She declared the idea of "bring your children to work day" obsolete for Gen Y. The reason? Statistics show that 30 percent of the current workforce is independently employed,[3] according to Working Today, a national nonprofit that advocates for the self-employed. Moreover, judging from recent trends, this statistic is probably on the rise.

Gen Y women say, however, that they don't want to opt out, i.e., leave the workforce, despite the recent media buzz about this trend. In fact, the 2006 Lifetime Women's Pulse Poll, which surveyed three generations of women, found that Gen Y women were the least likely to say they'd leave their career behind if they didn't need a paycheck. But almost two-thirds of Gen Y women said they'd rather start their own business than stay in their cur-

2. Quoted in ibid.
3. Courtney Martin, "Gen Y's Opt-out Vision," *Christian Science Monitor*, April 27, 2006. www.csmonitor.com/2006/0427/p09s02-coop.html

rent jobs, compared to half of boomers.[4] It's probably the reason why women-owned businesses grew 20 percent between 1997 and 2002, twice the national average for all businesses, according to a 2006 U.S. Census Bureau report.[5] In addition, American women start up almost five times as many new businesses as women in other high-income countries.[6] The numbers tell the story. Young women, and women in general, are increasingly finding traditional work environments unsatisfying and unrewarding, and are leaving to make a go of it on their own.

However, not everyone wants to—or can—pack it up to start her own medical practice, interior design firm, or private equity shop. Nor should we. Traditional jobs still account for the majority of employment opportunities. That is why the challenge in front of us young women is to figure how to make the workplace a better and more rewarding place. At the end of the day, what we want are choices—the choice to stay in a traditional work environment, and the choice to leave. What we don't want, though, is to feel as if we have to leave to escape the oppressive culture of the traditional workplace.

What many young women interviewed for this book say they found off-putting about the workplace, particularly when thinking about the long term, was the incompatibility warnings they had started to heed about marriage, children, and work. Take Molly who, entering her fourth year of medical school, says she was getting these kinds of incompatibility warnings at the ripe old

4. LifeTime Women's Pulse Poll. Researchers Kellyanne Conway and Celinda Lake Join LifeTime Television to Examine Differences Among Generation Y, Generation X and Baby Boomer Women. Press Release, March 27, 2006.
5. U.S. Census Bureau News, "Women-Owned Businesses Grew at Twice the National Average," January 26, 2006.
6. Joshua Holland, "Womenomics 101," Alternet.org, March 16, 2006. www.truthout.org/issues_06/031706WB.shtml

age of 24. "I was shocked by how many conversations people were having about how I was a woman, and that meant that I was going to be having children, and therefore I had to consider my career in terms of being home for them. I must have had five conversations with people saying things along the lines of, 'Molly, you might not realize it now, but it's going to factor in.' But never once was there a mention of the fact that you'll marry someone who will share the responsibility with you. It's all about me and *my* responsibility if I want to have kids." And you wonder why only 2 percent of Fortune 500 executives are women.

In a similar situation to Molly's, Heather, a software engineer, was questioned by her boss about her personal life. "I told him I had a boyfriend and he said, 'I hope I don't lose you when you get married and have children.' " Employers, understandably, are worried about turnover, which costs companies a lot of money, but why aren't employers asking, "What can we do to make it worthwhile for you to stay?" instead of, "What is your marriage and fertility timetable?

It seems, then, that the issue at hand is how young women can make work meaningful, lucrative, and satisfying in the early stages of their career. It's easier said than done, of course, but just imagine how different the workplace would be if young women thought about *building* careers instead of *finding* jobs, negotiated more aggressively for raises and salaries, tried to stay off the doormat track, built teams of mentors, and made a concerted effort to squelch all the catfights and competition with their female co-workers. Perhaps someday *Time, Newsweek,* and the latest trend piece in the *New York Times* will be talking about the *opt-in* revolution. Of course, change can't happen overnight, but if young women start thinking about these issues in the early stages of their career, 2 percent of women CEOs will continue to be the legacy of working women.

The Road Ahead

There are a number of positive changes happening for women in the workplace right now. And by making the environment better for women, we are making it better for everyone. Gene Sperling, in his book *The Pro-Growth Progressive*, cites a study of one hundred U.S. businesses that found that employees participating in a company's work–life programs were 45 percent more likely to say they'd go the extra mile for their employers than their colleagues who weren't in the program.[7] Sperling's conclusions aren't cryptic. As Alternet writer Joshua Holland sums them up, "Giving employees more flexibility results in improved 'motivation, making workers more productive' and reduces employee turnover." Now, why can't business heed such a simple lesson?

Some have: Firms like the accounting giant Deloitte and Touche have been able to promote and retain women by offering flexible working schedules, leadership development and career planning programs, and mentoring programs. Deloitte also maintains generous sabbatical policies and outreach practices so that women who depart the firm to raise children have an easier time reentering the work force. Still, when will all businesses, large and small, start taking notice of their *Jane Drain*, the phenomenon of women leaving a firm at a faster rate than men do?

A May 2003 article in *Barron's*, "Breaking the Glass: More Women Reach Top Spots, but Sexism Persists," takes the optimistic outlook that it's no longer a question of whether women will

7. Quoted in Holland, "Womenomics 101,"

be running a substantial share of corporate America, but when.[8] *Barron's* estimates that one in seven powerful posts will be held by women by 2010, based on evidence that the trend is growing strong. By 2020, it could be one in five.[9] Still those predictions are contingent on young women moving up through the workforce in the next two, five, and ten years.

Having Part of It All

Samantha Jones, the blond character who was always pushing the envelope with her racy remarks and sexual exploits on *Sex and the City*, famously yelled from the window of her recently purchased apartment in the trendy meatpacking district, "We have it all—great jobs, great apartments, great sex." Today's young women are trying to live up to the expectation that we can have the high-powered career, a great marriage, and be president of the PTA.

Casey, now a social work student, when reflecting on this expectation, disagreed. "I don't think any woman says, 'I have it all.' I don't think you can have it all. I think you can have part of it all. You can't be the head of a Fortune 500 company, an amazing partner, an amazing friend, and go to yoga class three times a week. But I really do see women having *part* of it all. I see women working and having partners and their partners are available to help shoulder more of the responsibility."

Judith Rodin, former president of the University of Pennsylvania and now president of the Rockefeller Foundation, says,

8. Gene Epstein, "Breaking the Glass: More women reach top spots, but sexism persists," *Barron's* May 24, 2003. www.women-unlimited.com/p_barrons_5-24-03.html.
9. Ibid.

"[Young people are] telling us they fear they can't have it all. I tell young women, 'You can have it all. Men do. What we want is the same range of choices that men have.' If women want to stay home, fine. If not, fine. But when we criticize those decisions, we make it harder for young women."[10]

To have one piece "of it all"—a satisfying career—consider taking a "me year," a year to focus on your career. Often in our quest to "have it all"—husband, baby, and job—by some random date (age 35 seems to be the new doomsday), we're often afraid to take any kind of time to figure out the type of career that is going to sustain us for the long haul. Many young women have become more consumed with a timetable but, at the end of the day, a timetable is just not as satisfying as a great career. We need to start asking ourselves at 22, 24, and 28, *Where do I want to be in my career in twenty years?*

Peggy Orenstein, in her book *Flux: Woman on Sex, Work, Love, Kids, and Life in a Half-Changed World* cites the research of sociologist Ann Machung, who interviewed seniors on six college campuses about their career aspirations. She concluded that woman saw work more as a vehicle of personal satisfaction than the way men saw it, as a money-making tool. Orenstein describes Machung's research like this: "Unlike the men, [women] reflexively factored inequality into their futures. They assumed that they would move in and out of the workforce and that family responsibilities would limit both their advancement and earning potential—but not their husband's. Seven out of ten said, once married, they expected their spouse's job to take priority. So well before they entered the adult world (and, perhaps, long before they'd entered college) young women were making decisions that

10. Quoted in Ann McFeatters, "Powerful Women in Washington Ask: Can We Have It All?" *Post-Gazette*, May 5, 2002.

would virtually assure that their careers would be secondary to men's and that their income would be lower . . ." As Machung wrote, they were talking "career," but thinking "job."[11]

However, the problem with thinking "job" versus "career" is that the vast majority of us will need a double-income household to maintain a middle-class lifestyle. In fact, many say that DINK (double income, no kids) should be placed with DINA (double income, need another). Life is expensive. To remedy this, Linda Hirshman, in her provocative 2005 article in *The American Prospect*, "Homeward Bound," says, "Women who want to have sex and children with men as well as good work in interesting jobs where they may occasionally wield real social power need guidance, and they need it early."[12]

Hirshman suggests that feminist organizations should produce a survey of the most common job opportunities for people with college degrees, along with the average lifetime earnings from each job category and the characteristics such jobs require. She says, "[We] need to help women see that yes, you can study art history, but only with the realistic understanding that one day soon you will need to use your arts education to support yourself and your family."[13] It doesn't need to be that extreme, but to boil that down to a rule, start thinking about how to use your college or graduate education with an eye to career goals.

As Candace Bushnell, the *New York Observer* writer whose column inspired *Sex and the City*, put it when commenting on the *Newsweek* retraction of its statement that a 40-year-old woman is more likely to be killed by a terrorist than married, "What we all

11. Peggy Orenstein, *Flux: Women on Sex, Work, Love, Kids, and Life in a Half-Changed World*. New York: Anchor Books, 2001, p. 19
12. Linda Hirshman, "Homeward Bound," *The American Prospect*, December 20, 2005.
13. Ibid.

need to understand is that career women are here to stay, and they're renegotiating the rules of relationships and marriages and motherhood."[14] Let's make sure we, as young women, keep renegotiating the rules, or we'll be stuck playing by the old ones. But the rules won't change on their own—they never do. Change is spawned by a movement, the type of movement that gave women the right to vote, entrance to the workplace, and access to birth control. To help start this movement, keep the following in mind—and, most important, in *collective* action.

14. Quoted in Jessica Yellin, "Single, Female and Desperate No More," *New York Times,* June 4, 2006.

TAKEAWAYS

- Focus the workplace discussion not on opting out, but on what employers can do to make it worth women's while to stay.

- Work with your female co-workers, so you'll have a collective muscle to flex when you need to lobby for change.

- You *can* have it all. Keep the words of Judith Rodin in mind: "You can have it all. Men do. What we want is the same range of choices that men have. If women want to stay home, fine. If not, fine. But when we criticize those decisions, we make it harder for young women."*

- Think "career" not "job." A career will ultimately be more meaningful, lucrative, and satisfying.

- Take a "me year," or just commit to taking a designated period of time to think about your career. Young women need to start asking themselves at 22, 25, 27, 31, and 33, *Where do I want to be in my* career *in twenty years?*

* McFeatters, "Powerful Women in Washington Ask: Can We Have It All?"

GLOSSARY

Active Listening – The act of listening to another person in a way that improves mutual understanding.

Assistant-ized – A situation in which a young woman employee gets trapped into doing all of the administrative work.

Background Check – A check you perform on the company with which you are interviewing, to assess its climate toward women. Some critical things to scope out: the number of women in managerial positions, avenues for mentoring, how fast other women at the company are advancing, lawsuits brought against the company for sexual harassment or discrimination, and any pay disparity that might exist.

The Back Story – In office politics, the background on a particular office dynamic that you aren't privy to because you are new on the job. Not knowing the back story is often the culprit for taking things too personally and other workplace misunderstandings.

Bank Account of Trust and Credit – The idea that trust among co-workers must evolve over time and build up in small increments. Before you divulge personal information to your co-workers, make sure you sure have a bank account of trust and credit in order to avoid placing your trust in the wrong people.

Career-Track Job – A career-track job is a job that helps you build toward the job you'd like to have in five, ten, or twenty years.

Commencement Castaways – What graduates become without proper guidance.

Contingency Plan – If you've become involved in an office romance, you should always develop a contingency, plan with your significant other in case the relationship doesn't work out. Essentially, it's an agreement of how you'll act at work if you break up.

Cover Yourself Tactics (CYT) – Strategies that will help you avert many office disasters, and look good to your boss and co-workers. For example, sending progress reports, double-checking paperwork, thinking beyond your job title, and following up.

Cubicle Etiquette – The unspoken rule of how to conduct yourself in your cubicle. Basics include: not speaking too loudly on your phone, not eating pungent foods, and generally being aware that you work in a small, open space.

An "Erin" – A woman in your peer group who takes you under her wing.

Face Time – Literally the amount of time co-workers see you in the office regardless of whether you are actually working or shopping on eBay.

Fear-Based Model – The reason many women stay in the wrong jobs too long—they are afraid they'll never find another job.

Fear of the Dumb Question – The fear women have of asking questions because they don't want to be a burden, or expose themselves as a weak employee.

The Generation Gap – The product of the influx of young women entering professions where they are working alongside co-workers of different generations.

Glass Ceiling – In 1991, the U.S. Department of Labor defined glass ceilings as "those artificial barriers based on attitudinal or organizational bias that prevent qualified individuals from advancing upward in their organization into management-level positions."

Going to Bat for Yourself – Taking action for yourself at work. For example, asking to be assigned to a specific project, a promotion, or a raise when no one offers it to you.

Integration – The concept that young women want to integrate all aspects of their personalities into the workplace.

Jane Drain – The phenomenon of women leaving a corporation at a faster rate than men do.

The Megillah – A system created by Ellie Cullman at her interior design firm, Cullman & Kravis, after she realized that employees were consistently making the same mistake. She implemented the equivalent of an office message board so that employees could develop an institutional memory, rather than each person just making the same mistake over and over again.

The New Girls' Network – A network of young women who help each other climb up the corporate ladder. Think what a twenty-year edge on networking would do for everyone's career!

No Triangling Rule – The act of being direct when a problem arises. If you are encountering a problem with a certain co-worker, you should approach that person to solve the problem, instead of going to a third party. This helps prevent office gossip and distrust.

The Old Boys' Club – An environment wherein men utilize their social connections to help other men climb the corporate ladder.

Outsource the Blame – When you don't take responsibility for something that goes wrong at the office in which you had direct involvement.

The Overqualified and Underappreciated Syndrome – Realizing that your job could probably be done by anyone and that you would make more money working as a camp counselor.

Paper Trail – Just what it sounds like: a trail of paper (real or virtual) documenting your work. It comes in handy when you need proof of correspondence, documentation of problems, or verification of facts.

The Power of Nice – A management technique introduced by Linda Kaplan Thalter and Robin Koval in their book, *The Power of Nice*, that has helped them become one of the fastest growing ad agencies in the country.

Progress Reports – Reports written regularly for your boss to let him/her know the status of your project(s).

The Psychology of Scarcity – The psychology that there isn't going to be enough room for women to advance together, the outgrowth of which can be a competitive and/or catty dynamic among women.

Putting on Earmuffs – The act of "covering your ears" to avoid being offended by everyday comments in a male-dominated workplace.

Sandbagged – When a boss decides to hurl a litany of complaints at you with little warning. This is a situation that is more likely to occur if you wait until your year-end review to get feedback, instead of asking for it from your boss on a more frequent basis.

The Second Revolution – The creation of a workplace that accommodates and appreciates the professional and personal needs of female employees. The first revolution came over thirty years ago when women first significantly entered the workplace.

Sense of Entitlement – The attitude projected by some members of Gen Y who feel they should bypass paying their dues and head straight to the executive suite.

Soft Skills – Those less-tangible skills, such as communication, creativity, analytical thinking, diplomacy, flexibility, and listening skills.

The Stay-Involved Approach – Staying involved means finding something valuable to do at the office—even if it's something as trivial as filing—rather than surfing the Net or reading a magazine.

Thick Skin – The acquired ability to let things (particularly criticism that isn't constructive) roll off your back and not take even the most negative comments personally.

Tiara Syndrome – A term coined by co-founders of Negotiating Women, Carol Frohlinger and Deborah Kolb. The idea that if you stay quiet and work hard, someone will put a tiara on your head, and give you a raise or promotion without prompting from you. Beware of this syndrome! The best way get what you want is to ask for it.

Thinking Bigger Picture – Understanding how the small, mundane tasks you are doing fit into the larger scheme of your organization or company—and your career.

Unperfect It – An approach recommended by Lorraine Lafferty, coauthor of *Perfectionism: A Sure Cure for Happiness* whereby you stop dwelling on the trivial details. To unperfect it, prioritize what needs extra attention and what doesn't.

Water Cooler Girl – The office gossip.

Why Is She Being Such a Bitch? – A common reaction toward a female co-worker or boss.

Workforce Depression – What many people new to the work-force experience as they mourn the loss of their carefree college days.

Work Martyr – The girl who works longer than everyone else when it's not necessary.

RESOURCES

Badbossology
A great resource for more advice on how to deal with a bad boss.
  www.badbossology.com

Catalyst
Catalyst is the leading research and advisory organization working with businesses and the professions to build inclusive environments and expand opportunities for women at work.
  www.catalystwomen.org

Coach Me, Inc.
Coach Me illuminates the subtle skills and unwritten rules necessary for advancement, nurtures initiative, and gives women the edge to maximize their individual potential and realize professional aspirations.
  www.coachmeinc.org

D. A. Hayden and Wilder, Career Counselors
Hayden Wilder provides counsel to people starting out, 98 percent of whom land in career-track jobs.
  www.haydenwilder.com

David Swink, Human Resources Consultant

A well-known human resources firm that focuses on diversity, preventing school/workplace violence, sexual harassment, developing emotional intelligence, relationship management, conflict resolution, leadership development and coaching, visioning, team building, and other important workplace issues.

www.strategicinteractions.com

Debra Lindquist, Image Consultant

A great resource on what and what not to wear to the office.

www.lindquistassociates.com

Dr. Judith Briles

Dr. Judith Briles's site addresses issues of confidence, change, and sabotage in the workplace.

www.briles.com

Gail Evans

Best-selling author of career bibles, *Play Like a Man, Win Like a Woman* and *She Wins, You Win*.

www.gailevans.net

Judi Perkins, Find the Perfect Job

Judi Perkins, a career consultant with two decades of experience, offers valuable resources and advice about finding a job you won't want to quit.

www.findtheperfectjob.com

Linda Hirshman

A provocative and informative site that offers a Plan to Get to Work (also the title of Hirshman's 2005 book, *Get to Work: A Manifesto for Women of the World*), through education strategic planning, and the right family planning.

www.gettoworkmanifesto.com

Martha Burk, Women's Rights Expert and Author of Cult of Power

www.marthaburk.org/index.html

My Toxic Boss

Provides strategies and resources for targets of workplace bullying.

www.mytoxicboss.com

Nan Mooney, Author of I Can't Believe She Did That

I Can't Believe She Did That offers a new and compelling perspective on conflict and competition among women in the workplace.

www.nanmooney.com

National Organization for Women

The National Organization for Women (NOW) is the largest organization of feminist activists in the United States.

www.now.org

Negotiating Women

Negotiating Women, Inc., is a company of women committed to helping other women recognize that performance doesn't speak for itself.

www.negotiatingwomen.com

The Power of Nice

Linda Kaplan Thaler and Robin Koval have moved to the top of the advertising industry by following a simple but powerful philosophy: It pays to be nice.

www.thepowerofnice.com

Quarterlife Crisis

A one-stop shop for recent grads and beyond for navigating everything from your career to finances to your social life.

www.quarterlifecrisis.com

Rachel Simmons, Author of Odd Girl Out:
The Hidden Culture of Aggression in Girls

Rachel Simmons is the author of the *New York Times* best-seller *Odd Girl Out: The Hidden Culture of Aggression in Girls*, the first book to explore the phenomenon of bullying among girls.

www.rachelsimmons.com

Simmons School of Management

A leading center for innovative teaching, research and discourse on women, leadership and management, the School of Management (SOM) offers a demanding management education to women MBA and undergraduate students. SOM is also a leading-edge provider of executive education, consulting services, and applied research to senior management in business, government, and the nonprofit sector.

www.simmons.edu/com

They Don't Teach Corporate in College: A Twenty-Something's Guide to the Business World

Based on a mix of interviews, research and the author, Alexandra Levit's personal journey, *They Don't Teach Corporate in College* offers great advice for any twentysomething.

www.corporateincollege.com

Women Don't Ask: Negotiation and the Gender Divide

Based on their book of the same title, Linda Babcock and Sara Laschever's site offers a plethora of insightful material about women and negotiation.

www.womendontask.com

Women for Hire

Founded in 1999 by Tory Johnson as the first and only company devoted to a comprehensive array of recruitment services for women, Women for Hire offers signature career expos, inspiring speeches and seminars, a popular career-focused magazine, customized marketing programs, and an online job board that help leading employers connect with top-notch professional women in all fields.

www.womenforhire.com

Women Unlimited

Since 1994, Women Unlimited has partnered with top organizations to help attract, retain and develop emerging, high-potential, and executive women. Founder, Jean Otte, is also the author of *Changing the Corporate Landscape: A Woman's Guide to Cultivating Leadership Excellence.*

www.women-unlimited.com

Woodhull Institute

The Woodhull Institute is a not-for-profit, nonpartisan, nonsectarian educational organization that provides ethical leadership training and professional development for women.

woodhull.org

Younger Women's Task Force

A grassroots movement for young women.

www.ywtf.org

INDEX